James Macpherson

The Rights of Great Britain Asserted against the Claims of America

Being an Answer to the Declaration of the General Congress

James Macpherson

The Rights of Great Britain Asserted against the Claims of America
Being an Answer to the Declaration of the General Congress

ISBN/EAN: 9783337232061

Printed in Europe, USA, Canada, Australia, Japan

Cover: Foto ©Suzi / pixelio.de

More available books at **www.hansebooks.com**

THE RIGHTS

OF

GREAT BRITAIN ASSERTED

AGAINST THE

CLAIMS OF AMERICA:

BEING AN

ANSWER

TO THE

DECLARATION

OF THE

GENERAL CONGRESS.

THE THIRD EDITION,
WITH ADDITIONS.

LONDON:

ADVERTISEMENT.

THE materials upon which the following Pamphlet is formed, were derived from the best and most incontestible authorities. The Author had access to original papers, accurate estimates, and authentic dispatches. He has also availed himself of the records of both Houses of Parliament; and he has made it his business to examine, with attention, such printed tracts as might contribute to throw any light on the subject. Upon the whole, more labour and time have been employed on this short disquisition, than are generally bestowed upon fugitive Publications of the same kind. The design of the Writer has been to extricate the contest now subsisting between Great-Britain and her Colonies, from the errors of the ignorant, and the misrepresentations of designing men. As he has rigidly adhered to truth throughout, and to such arguments as naturally arise from undoubted facts, he hopes he has attained his object.

AN ANSWER

TO THE

DECLARATION

OF THE

GENERAL CONGRESS.

WHEN Independent States take up arms, they endeavour to imprefs the World with a favourable opinion of their own caufe, and to lay the blame of hoftilities on the injuftice of their Opponents. But if Nations, accountable to none for their conduct, deem it neceffary to reconcile others to their proceedings, the neceffity is ftill more urgent with regard to thofe who, breaking through every political duty, draw their fwords againft the State of which they own themfelves the Subjects. The opinions of mankind are invariably oppofed to fuch men. Their affertions are heard with diftruft, their arguments weighed

weighed with caution; and, therefore, it is as neceſſary for THEM to adhere to truth, in the former, as it is prudent to avoid ſophiſtry in the latter.

This conſideration, however obvious it may appear to others, ſeems to have totally eſcaped the attention of the body of men who lately ſat at Philadelphia under the name of " The General " American Congreſs." In a paper publiſhed under the title of " A DECLARATION by the Repreſentatives of the United Colonies of North " America" *, the facts are either wilfully or ignorantly miſrepreſented; and the arguments deduced from premiſes that have no foundation in truth. But, as whatever falls from men who call themſelves the Repreſentatives of a People, muſt fall with ſome degree of weight on the minds of the undiſcerning part of mankind; it becomes, in ſome meaſure, neceſſary to examine briefly the reaſons held forth by the Congreſs to juſtify the rebellion of their Conſtituents. On a ſubject ſo trite, arguments advanced by other Writers may ſometimes recur; but novelty is leſs the object of this part of the diſquiſition, than perſpicuity and preciſion.

The Declaration of the Congreſs begins with an involved period, which either contains no meaning, or a meaning not founded on the prin-

---

* Vide Appendix.

ciples of reason. They seem to infinuate, that no body of men, in any Empire, can exercife "an "unbounded authority over others;" an opinion contrary to fact under every form of Government. No maxim in policy is more univerfally admitted, than that a fupreme and uncontroulable power muft exift fomewhere in every State. This ultimate power, though juftly dreaded and reprobated in the perfon of ONE MAN, is the firft fpring in every Political Society. The great difference, between the degrees of freedom in various Governments, confifts merely in the manner of placing this neceffary difcretionary power. In the Britifh Empire it is vefted, where it is moft fafe, in King, Lords, and Commons, under the collective appellation of the Legiflature. The Legiflature is another name for the Conftitution of the State; and, in fact, the State itfelf. The Americans ftill own themfelves the fubjects of the State; but if they refufe obedience to the laws of the Legiflature, they play upon words, and are no longer Subjects, but Rebels. In vain have they affirmed that they are the Subjects of the King's prerogative, and not his Subjects in his legiflative quality; as the King, with regard to his Subjects in general, is to be confidered only in his executive capacity as the great hereditary Magiftrate, who carries into effect the laws of the Legiflature, the

only

only discretionary and uncontroulable power in a free State.

The discretionary and uncontroulable authority of the British Legislature being granted, their right to tax all the Subjects of the British Empire can never be denied. Some ill-informed reasoners in politics have lately started an obsolete maxim, which has been seized with avidity by the Americans, That " the Supreme Power cannot take " from any one any part of his property without " his consent;" or in other words, That Representation is inseparable from Taxation. The Colonists, say they, have no Representatives in Parliament, and therefore Parliament has no right to tax the Colonists. Upon this principle, scarce one in twenty-five of the people of Great-Britain is represented. Out of more than seven millions, fewer than three hundred thousand have an exclusive right to chuse Members of Parliament; and, therefore, more than three times the number of the Americans have an equal right with them to dispute the authority of the Legislature to subject them to taxes. The truth is, Representation never accompanied Taxation in any State. The Romans were a free nation; yet the Senate, that is, the great body of the Nobility, possessed the sole right of taxing the people. In this kingdom, the

House

House of Commons have an exclusive right of modifying and regulating the quantity of public supplies, and the manner of laying taxes: but the Commons, by their own authority, cannot enforce the raising the supplies they vote. That privilege is inherent in the supreme and unaccountable power vested in the three branches of the Legislature united; who are in fact the State, as the virtual Representatives of the whole Empire, and not the delegates of individuals.

Why it has been so generally received as a maxim, in this country, That Taxation and Representation are inseparable, requires to be explained. Men, little acquainted with the Constitution, derived the opinion from their finding, that it is the indisputable right of the Commons, that all grants of subsidies and parliamentary aids should originate in their House. But though they first bestow those subsidies and aids, their grants, as has been already observed, have no effect without the assent of the other two branches of the Legislature. The common reason given for this exclusive privilege is, That as the supplies are raised upon the body of the people, the people only ought to have the right of taxing themselves. This argument would have been conclusive, if the Commons taxed none but those by whose whofe fuffrages they obtained their feats in Parliament. But it has appeared, that more than feven millions of people, befides the Peers, who are in poffeffion of fo large a fhare of property in the kingdom, have no voice in the election of the Members who fit in the Lower Houfe. The Commons, therefore, and their Conftituents not being the *only* perfons taxed, the former cannot poffibly have the *only* right of raifing and modelling the fupply, from the mere circumftance of Reprefentation. But if they have it not from Reprefentation, they muft in fact derive it from the fupreme and difcretionary power, which is repofed in them, in conjunction with the two other branches of the Legiflature. It appears, upon the whole, that Taxation is the refult of the difcretionary power which is placed in the hands of the Legiflature, and exerted by them for the neceffary fupport of the State. To this power the whole Empire muft submit, and confequently no one of its fubjects can claim any exemption.

The Counties Palatine of Chefter, Durham, and Lancafter, were anciently in the fame predicament with the Americans, on the article of Taxation. The Earl of Chefter and the Bifhop of Durham became, by prefcription and immemorial cuftom, poffeffed of a kind of regal

regal jurifdiction, within their refpective territories. A fimilar form of Government was eftablifhed by King Edward III. in the County of Lancafter; which was erected firft into an Earldom, and then into a Dukedom, in the perfon of Henry Plantagenet; whofe heirefs carried the fame rights and privileges to John of Gant, that King's fourth fon, and his pofterity. But though the SUBORDINATE SOVEREIGNS of thefe Counties could pardon treafons, murders and felonies; though they appointed all Judges, nominated all Juftices of the Peace, and, in fhort, poffeffed exclufively the whole internal Government of their feveral Counties; their SUBJECTS (if the expreffion may be ufed) were "al-
" ways bound by the Acts and Statutes" * of an Affembly, in which they had no Reprefentatives. They were alfo " liable to all payments, rates, and
" fubfidies, granted by the Parliament of Eng-
" land" †.

Thofe Counties (it muft be confeffed), like the Americans, confidered their being excluded from having Reprefentatives in an Affembly by which they were taxed, a grievance. Accordingly, the

---

* Statutes at Large, 34 and 35 of Henry VIII. c. 13.
† Ibid. 25 of Charles II. c. 9.

Town and County of Chester, as far back as the thirty-fifth of Henry VIII. petitioned the Legislature for the privilege of sending Members to Parliament; and their request was granted by an express Statute *. The County and City of Durham made a similar application, and with the same success, in the twenty-fifth of Charles II †. Had the Americans, instead of flying to arms, submitted the same supposed grievance, in a peaceable and dutiful manner, to the Legislature, I can perceive no reason why their request should be refused. Had they, like the County and City of Chester, represented, that " for lack of Knights and Bur-
" gesses to represent them in the High Court of
" Parliament, they had been oftentimes TOUCHED
" and GRIEVED with Acts and Statutes made with-
" in the said Court, derogatory to their most an-
" cient jurisdictions, liberties and privileges, and
" prejudicial to their quietness, rest and peace;" this Country would, I am persuaded, have no objection to their being represented in her Parliament.

But the Colonies, though that circumstance is only insinuated in the Declaration, have uniformly affirmed, that granting the supremacy of Parlia-

---

* 34 and 35 of Henry VIII. c. 13.

† 25 of Charles II. c. 9,

ment

ment should extend over the whole Empire, yet that they themselves have a right to an exemption from Taxes either by the conceſſions of the Legiſlature, or by charters from the King. It ſeems incompatible with reaſon, ſay they, that the Colonies ſhould have internal Legiſlatures of their own, poſſeſſing the authority of taxation, and that, notwithſtanding, the Britiſh Parliament ſhould retain its power of laying impoſts. The firſt of theſe aſſertions is not founded in truth. The Charters give no exemption from Taxation: on the contrary, ſome of them, for inſtance the Charter of Pennſylvania, expreſsly ſubjects the inhabitants of that Province to the payment of "ſuch "taxes as were then (in 1680) laid, or ſhould "thereafter be laid on America, by the Par- "liament of England." But had the Charters mentioned an exemption, the Legiſlature, by virtue of its ſupreme, univerſal, and diſcretionary power, can recal any rights they have conferred, when the good of the State renders that meaſure neceſſary. Though the King may give away by Charter a right that militates againſt himſelf, as hereditary Chief Magiſtrate, he cannot authorize, by any deed whatever, an exemption from the general laws of the State. In ſuch a caſe ONE of the THREE branches of the Legiſlature would uſurp the power of the THREE UNITED; a

C   ſolecism

solecism as great in polity, as it is in mathematicks to affirm, that a part is greater than the whole.

It may be neceffary, perhaps, to make an apology for entering fo minutely into the argument in favour of the right of Taxation. The Americans themfelves have deferted that ground. They fpeak no longer as fubjects. They affume the language of rivals, and they act as enemies. The queftion between them and Great-Britain (for it is no longer between them and Government) confifts of dependence or independence, connection or no connection, except on the footing of a Sovereign State. They have already arrogated to themfelves all the functions of Sovereignty. They have formed a great deliberative Council. They have taken the whole executive power into their own hands. They have ftruck a new currency, raifed armies, appointed generals ; and that they have not chofen ANOTHER SOVEREIGN, muft be afcribed more to their Republican principles, than to any remains of loyalty for their lawful Prince.

In this fituation of affairs and opinions, it is matter of little furprize, that men who deny the authority of the State should load the Legiflature with opprobrious epithets. The Congrefs accordingly ftigmatize Parliament with various charges of tyranny,

tyranny, violence, and oppreſſion. Paſſing from this ſtrain of general ſcurrility, they enter into warm encomiums on the anceſtors of their Conſtituents. But they now deviate as much from truth in their applauſe, as they had done before in their cenſure. They affirm, that the anceſtors of the Coloniſts obtained the lands which they have tranſmitted to the preſent race, "without any charge "to the country from which they removed." Their very enemies could not wiſh to meet them on more advantageous ground. The ſums expended upon the various Provinces, ſince their firſt eſtabliſhment, for their ordinary ſupport, government, and protection, have been ſo enormous, that without the authority of inconteſtible vouchers, they could ſcarcely obtain credit *.

---

* *An Account of what Sums have been granted to the different Provinces in* North America, *as far as it appears from the Eſtimates for the ſupport of the Civil Government of each Province; and alſo what Sums have been granted for the Support of the Provincial Forces in* North America.

	£.	s.	d.
New York Forces	339,055	16	8
Carolina in general	43,024	9	10½
Georgia ſettling, and ſecuring that Province	250,853	4	6
——— Military Expence of ditto	130,066	18	4½
South Carolina Forces	101,524	5	6
Nova Scotia Civil Government	1,358,240	17	6½
Eaſt Florida Civil Government	59,300	0	0
Weſt Florida Civil Government	64,324	13	6
America in general forces	172,999	0	0
Rewards and compenſations	1,316,511	1	5
	3,835,900	7	4½

But, even granting that the Colonists had obtained their lands without any charge to the Mother-country, were they capable of keeping those lands without her assistance? Was it not to defend the Americans, that Great-Britain involved herself in the last expensive war? Did not those very "United Provinces," who now pretend to set the power of this Kingdom at defiance, lay themselves in the dust at her feet, to claim her aid and protection against a SINGLE Colony? Did they not complain in the same abject terms with the Britons of old, "That the Barbarians drove "them into the sea, and that the sea drove them "back on the Barbarians?" Did not Great-Britain, like a Guardian Angel, stretch forth her hand to their aid; and, by expelling their enemies from the Continent of America, rescue them, not only from danger, but the very fear of danger? Did she not, over and above the many millions she expended upon the fleets and armies employed in defence of the Colonies, advance more than ONE MILLION to pay THEIR own native forces, employed in THEIR own Cause †?

---

† GRANTS in PARLIAMENT for Rewards, Encouragement, and Indemnification to the Provinces in North America for their Services and Expences during the last War.
Date of Votes.

3 Febr. 1756. As a free Gift and Reward to the Colonies of New-England, New-York, and Jersey, for their past services,

Did not the Mother-country, with more than a mother's fondness, upon all occasions nourish, cherish,

Date of Votes.		£.	s.	d.
3 Febr. 1756.	and as an encouragement to them to continue to exert themselves with vigour, &c.	115,000	—	—
19 May, 1757.	For the use and relief of the Provinces of North and South Carolina and Virginia, in recompence for services performed and to be performed with the approbation of the Commander in Chief in America, - - - - -	50,000	—	—
1 June, 1758.	To reimburse the Province of Massachuset's Bay their expences in furnishing provisions and stores to the troops raised by them in 1756, £: 27,380 19 11½ To reimburse the Province of Connecticut their expences for ditto, £. 13,736 17 7	41,117	17	6¼
30 Apr. 1759.	As a compensation to the respective Colonies in North America for the expence of levying, cloathing and pay of the troops raised by them, &c.	200,000	—	—
31 Mar. 1760.	Ditto, - - -	200,000	—	—
	To the Colony of New York to reimburse their expences in furnishing provisions and stores to the troops raised by them in 1756 - -	2,977	7	8
		609,095	5	2¼

rish, and support this prodigal child, that left the house of his parent, "to feed on husks, "with the swine of the desart?" Has she not (to sum up the whole in one point of view) uniformly protected the Colonies in war, encouraged their produce with bounties in time of peace ‡, entered into

	£.	s.	d.
Brought over,	609,095	5	2¼
20 Jan. 1761. As a Compensation to the respective Colonies in North America, for the expence of levying, cloathing, and pay of the troops raised by them, &c.	200,000	—	—
26 Jan. 1762. Ditto,	133,333	6	8
15 Mar. 1763. Ditto,	133,333	6	8
22 Apr. 1770. To reimburse the Province of New Hampshire their expences in furnishing provisions and stores to the troops raised by them for the Campaign in 1756	6,009	13	3
	1,081,771	11	9½

‡ *An Account of Bounties on* American *Commodities.*

	£.	s.	d.
Bounty on Indico from 1749 to 1773 paid by Great Britain	145,022	3	4¼
Bounty on Hemp and Flax paid under the Act of 4 Geo. III. ch. 26. from 1766 to 1772	5,560	8	7¾
Bounty on Importation of Naval Stores from America, pursuant to the Act of the 3d of Queen Anne, from 1706 to 1729	430,178	4	6
Under the Act of 2d Geo. II. from 1729 to 1774	1,028,584	7	3

Besides other Bounties granted on
    Raw Silk
    Pipe Staves
    Hogshead Staves
    Barrel Staves
    Pipe, Hogshead, or Barrel-Heading.

into all their quarrels with their neighbours, made their enemies her own; and, for their fake, has fhe not, in fome degree, fubjected herfelf to an annual tribute to Indian favages, in whom habitual injuries had raifed an irreconcileable hatred to their oppreffors? Did fhe not, too fatally, relinquifh great advantages on every other fide of a fuccefsful war, to eradicate the very feeds of future contefts in America; and, by giving the Colonies unlimited fecurity from ABROAD, procure for them that profperity at HOME, which has encouraged them, like parricides, to raife the dagger againft her own breaft?

The Congrefs, in the next paragraph of their Declaration, affect to reprobate the laft Peace, though they have derived fo many and fo great advantages from that treaty. The conduct of the Americans ought alfo to induce this Kingdom to regret the ftipulations fhe made for their fecurity. Had Canada remained in the hands of the French, the Colonies would have remained dutiful fubjects. Their fears for themfelves, in that cafe, would have fupplied the place of their pretended affection for this Nation. They would have fpoken more fparingly of their own refources, as they might daily ftand in need of our aid. Their former incapacity of defending themfelves would have always recurred to their minds, as

long

long as the objects of their former terror should continue so near their borders. But their habitual fears from France were, it seems, removed only to give room to their ingratitude to Great-Britain.

The effrontery with which the Congress reprobate the late Peace, is scarcely equal to their folly in applauding the Minister who had carried on the war. With peculiar inconsistency they affect to commence an æra of "Public Ruin," from Mr. Pitt's resignation in 1761; yet the whole "object of their wishes" is to be placed on the same footing as in the year 1763. They do not recollect, or rather they pretend to forget, that the most splendid actions in the war, happened after Mr. Pitt retired from his office. They are ignorant, or designedly conceal, that the commerce of this kingdom has amazingly encreased, and, in consequence, its revenue, since the æra from which they date public ruin. They know, or they ought, from their own experience, to know, that notwithstanding their shutting their ports against our manufactures, permanent and profitable sources of commerce have been opened in other quarters; that instead of being distressed by their present interruption to trade, our Merchants find themselves incapable of fulfilling their commissions from foreign states; that as

the

the fureft teft of the flourifhing condition of commerce, the courfe of exchange, to the amount of feveral per cents. is univerfally in favour of Great-Britain; and that, as the ultimate and invincible proof of the public profperity, the confidence of the people in the meafures of Government, and their contempt for the rebellious efforts of the refractory Colonies, the national Stocks fuffer neither fluctuation nor fall in the price.

Having reprefented the pretended ruin brought upon the Britifh Empire by the late Peace, the Congrefs defcend to the fictitious grievances of America fince the fame period. They affirm, that " the Colonies were judged to be in fuch a " ftate, as to prefent victories without bloodfhed, " and all the eafy emoluments of ftatutable " plunder." This figure of rhetoric, if it has any meaning, conveys one contrary to the truth. The Colonifts having obtained fuch amazing advantages by a Peace, which they now reprobate, it was deemed juft and proper by Mr. Grenville, then at the head of the Treafury, that they fhould bear a proportionable fhare of the national burdens incurred by the war. But as their prior inability to bear internal Taxes had precluded him from having a precedent, he only *threw out*, as it is vulgarly expreffed, in the beginning of the year 1764, his intentions of raifing a revenue in America by a Stamp-Duty, similar to that established in Great-Britain; referring the consideration of the whole affair to the next Session. His object was, to give time to the Colonies to propose some other mode of Taxation, should that suggested to Parliament appear either improper or burdensome. During the whole of the summer 1764, though some discontented spirits murmured, not a single doubt was started against the ABSOLUTE RIGHT of Parliament to impose Taxes on every Member of the British Empire. The time allowed to the Colonies furnished them with no expedient for raising a tax more suitable to the purpose of a Revenue (which, by the bye, was to have been spent among themselves); and, therefore, in the beginning of the year 1765, the famous Stamp-Act was passed, against a very inconsiderable Minority, in both Houses of Parliament.

In this Kingdom, as well as in every State possessed of freedom, there are always to be found factious persons, who oppose every measure of Government. In their eagerness to disgrace the Minister, they too frequently obstruct the service, and defeat the interests of their Country. Every side of a speculative point is armed with arguments, that may impose on the ignorant, and encourage the sanguine. The Opposition in Parliament, in short, committed themselves too far in favour of the prejudices of the Americans, with regard to the Stamp-Act, to support it with vigour, when they themselves, very unexpectedly*, came into Office, a few months after it had passed into Law. Though their view of the object changed with their elevation, they found that the flame which their own factious speeches, in the preceding Session, had raised in America, was too vehement to be extinguished without either force or concessions. A natural timidity of disposition, joined to the common want of firmness which accompanies novelty in Office, rendered them inclinable to purchase present quiet for themselves, at the expence of the future advantage of their Country. But still they wavered on the point of irresolution, till Mr. Pitt's oratory weighed down the scale. The Stamp-Act was repealed; and from that moment may be dated " the commencement of " what the Americans call " an Æra of Public " Ruin."

Great Britain and her Colonies derive their present dispute, and its consequent misfortunes, from the PATRIOTISM of the motley Junto who formed the appearance of an Administration, in the end of

---

* Lord Rockingham and others in Opposition came into office July 10, 1765, Grenville and his party having thrown themselves out of place on the Regency Bill.

1765 and beginning of 1766. Virginia had the MÉRIT of taking the lead in the disturbances in America, which succeeded the passing of the Stamp-Act. It was in the Assembly of that Province, that the first Resolutions were voted against the authority of Parliament, in the first Session, after intelligence of the Act was received. Though the meeting was very thin, the Resolutions passed only by a majority of TWO VOTES; and they would have been most certainly rejected, had it not been for the absence of forty of the old Members. When the Assembly was adjourned for the season, the people in general were dissatisfied with the conduct of their representatives. Every one expected, that, at the next meeting, an attempt would be made to eraze the Resolutions from the Journals. But intelligence arrived, in the mean time, that the Marquis of Rockingham, Lord Camden, General Conway, and the rest of the " illustrious Band" who had opposed the Stamp-Act in Parliament, were, by a strange revolution in politics, received into favour, and raised to office; and that Mr. Pitt, then at variance with his wife's relations, was resolved to oppose their FAVOURITE MEASURE, the Stamp-Act. The Virginians, deriving great hopes from this change, adhered to their Resolutions; and nothing further was done in the matter.

To

To enter minutely into the various motives of Mr. Pitt's oratory, for the total and absolute repeal of the Stamp-Act, would be to desert a great and public subject for the sake of tracing the private passions and interested views of an ambitious man. In his Argument, if what he advanced deserves the name, he fell in with the vulgar and, it may be said, false maxim, That no profit ought to be expected from the Colonies, but That resulting from their Commerce. This opinion of Mr. Pitt, whether it proceeded from ignorance or design (and it probably proceeded from both), has formed a popular error in former times, as well as in the present age. Many, who have pretended to understand perfectly the affairs of this Kingdom, most firmly, but in my opinion very weakly, believed, that the great secret of our political interest consisted in forcing, in a manner, a monopoly of foreign commerce. It was from this persuasion, that the popular Orator used, upon the occasion just mentioned, a figure of rhetoric at once foolish and absurd, when he affirmed, that the Colonists should be prohibited " from manufacturing even the hobnail of a horse-shoe!" One might be tempted to ask the Orator, how this prohibitory mandate could be enforced; or if it could, whether it is less arbitrary, than to demand an *internal* tax from the Americans, for the support of their own government,

ment, and even for the general support of the State, and as a suitable return for the protection which they have ever derived from the Government of this kingdom?

The Congress had surely forgot this strange rhetorical figure of the great Orator, when they were tempted to date PUBLIC RUIN, from his resignation in 1761. They have also forgot, or they do not chuse to remember, that he acquiesced in the DECLARATORY BILL, brought in and passed by the Marquis of Rockingham's Party, who were in office, in the beginning of the year 1766. This Bill expresly declares, " that all his Majesty's Colonies and Plantations in " America have been, are, and of right ought to " be, subordinate to and dependent upon the Im- " perial Crown and PARLIAMENT OF GREAT " BRITAIN; who have full power and authority " to make laws and statutes of sufficient validity to " bind the Colonies and People of America, sub- " jects of the Crown of Great Britain, IN ALL " CASES WHATSOEVER."

Mr. Pitt, to preserve some degree of consistency, objected to the words " IN ALL CASES WHATSO- EVER." But his opposition was so languid, that he did not attend the House when the Bill was passed;

paſſed; and only five Peers were found to follow his opinion, when it came under debate in the Houſe of Lords.

"The Declaratory Act," as the American Congreſs affirms, " comprehends all the grievances of which " they complain." Yet that very Congreſs, with peculiar effrontery, not only approve, but even praiſe the conduct of the very Party by whom the Bill was introduced, and the MAN, by whoſe CRIMINAL ACQUIESCENCE (to uſe one of his own phraſes) it paſſed into a law. THAT Party and THAT MAN, being now in oppoſition to Government, the Americans endeavour to ſecure their ſupport, by flattering their vanity at the expence of truth! They forget paſt demerits in the hopes of preſent ſervices. But when they expect to deceive a whole Party into their intereſt, they themſelves are made the tools of that Party; and, like the figure of the Negro, near Temple-bar, are turned round by the machine, which they pretend to move.

The Congreſs, in a ſtrain of eloquent adulation, ſpeaks with raptures of " that illuſtrious Band of " diſtinguiſhed Peers and Commoners," who now declaim, argue, and proteſt, in favour of their own Rebellion. It has appeared that the Act of which they moſt complain, was the manufacture of that
very

very "illustrious Band," encouraged by the negative opposition made by the Earl of Chatham, whose advice the Band followed, as it soon after appeared, to their own political destruction. Besides, was it not under the Administration of the Earl of Chatham, in the years 1767 and 1768, though the Americans date their misfortunes from the resignation of Mr. Pitt in October 1761, that the Bills imposing internal duties, and consequently establishing internal Taxation in America, were passed into laws *? Did not the present Administration, whose measures the Congress affect to reprobate throughout, repeal all those Acts, except the duty on Tea †, to gratify the prejudices of the Americans, and, if possible, to re-establish tranquility in all the Provinces? With what colour of reason, therefore, can the Americans lay the blame either of their real or pretended grievances on the Noblemen and Gentlemen now in office; and yet approve of the conduct of those very persons who passed the Declaratory Act, and followed it with Bills of imposts raised in the Colonies?

In reprobating the Declaratory Act, the Congress recur to their usual maxim, That Taxation

---

* 7 Geo. III. Ch. 46.
† 10 Geo. III.

and

and Reprefentation are infeparable. Though it has been already fhewn, that they are as much reprefented as twenty-four in twenty-five of the inhabitants of Great-Britain; though it has been proved, that whole Provinces, not reprefented, had been for feveral ages fubjected to impofts laid by the Legiflature; though it fhall, hereafter, appear that they themfelves have been uniformly taxed by the Britifh Parliament; this argument they hold forth as invincible, and found upon it their prefent refiftance to the fupremacy of the Parent-kingdom. In pyrfuing it injudicioufly and too far, they actually difcover the expediency, and even neceffity of that fupremacy, of which they fo loudly complain. The Parliament of Great-Britain, fay they, will certainly perceive, "that an American "revenue, if not diverted from the oftenfible "purpofes for which it is raifed, will actually "lighten their own burdens, in proportion as they "increafe ours." But is it not equitable, is it not juft, is it not neceffary, that all the fubjects of the empire fhould bear, as equally as poffible, the public burdens of the empire? Why fhould the Americans, who have fo largely, fo uniformly, and fo effectually experienced the protection of Government, be the only perfons exempted from paying their fhare of its expences? Is it either reafonable or fuitable to the common ufage of Nations,

tions, that those who desert their country should enjoy greater privileges than those that remain? The Americans having been spared during the infancy of their Colonies on account of their poverty, endeavour to establish into an inherent right what was actually an indulgence.

Though this indulgence has been a source of error to the more ignorant part of the Americans, there are surely many among them who know, that Parliament hath been uniformly accustomed to extend its supremacy over all the Colonies. In matters of revenue, in commerce, in civil, in all judicial regulations; and, in short, with regard to the general constitution of their government, the Provinces of North-America, till taught otherwise by a disappointed Faction in this Kingdom, allowed, that the whole fabrick of their polity might be new-modelled and reformed by the superintending power of Parliament. In fact, it has been so new-modelled and reformed, whenever abuses in the Administration of their Government, under their civil polity, or the general interest of the British Empire, made it necessary for Parliament to interpose its authority. Instances of this interposition, in both cases, present themselves, in almost every volume of the Statutes, from the Restoration down to the present reign; yet the Americans falsely insinuate, that it was in the present reign

reign the exercife of the authority of Parliament (except only in the regulation of trade) firft commenced.

A brief recital of fome of thofe inftances may throw light on a fubject, rendered obfcure and perplexed by the prejudices of the ignorant, and the arts of defigning men. To gain the ears of the Populace, by awakening their ancient jealoufies, the Americans affect to afcribe the prefent fyftem of meafures to principles of Toryifm, which, they pretend, prevail in our Councils. But, unfortunately for this part of their plan of deception, it will appear, that moft of the Acts which bind America in coercive regulations, were paffed foon after the Revolution; in the reign of the very Prince, who brought about that great event. The Whig Minifters of King William (perceiving that the Colonies, even then, had entertained views of placing themfelves on a ground of independence on Parliament) advifed their Sovereign, and their advice now ftands on record, to purfue. meafures, which, in their confequence, fhould effectually fecure their thorough dependence on the Legiflature of this Kingdom.

In confequence of the advice given by a Whig Miniftry to a King who had mounted the throne upon WHIG principles; and also upon the fullest evidence of the frauds and abuses committed in the Plantations, in violation of the Act of Navigation; the Act of the 7th and 8th of William III. " for preventing frauds, and regulating abuses, in " the Plantations" was passed. By that Act, a power was given to the Commissioners of the Treasury and Customs in England, " to establish ports, " and appoint Officers, in the Plantations; and " those Officers to have the same authority for " visiting ships and goods, and entering houses " and warehouses, as was exercised by the same " Officers in England."

All penalties and forfeitures were made recoverable in the Courts at Westminster, or in Courts of Admiralty, in the Plantations; which Courts were then, for the *first time*, established throughout all America. In any action or suit concerning his Majesty's Duties, the offence might be laid in any precinct or division of the Plantations, where the same should be alledged to have been committed, at the discretion of the Officer or Informer. All laws, by-laws, usages and customs repugnant to any laws of Great Britain which relate to the Plantations, or mention the same, are declared " illegal, null, and void." Many other restrictions, too

too tedious to be mentioned, were at the fame time enacted and impofed.

But it was not in matters of Trade ONLY, that Parliament, during the reign of King William, fuperintended and controuled the Colonies, The Coloniſts, it was found, had encouraged Pirates, in various places; and no juſtice could be obtained in THEIR Courts againſt offenders, whom they openly abetted. To remedy this fhameful abufe, a remarkable Act was paſſed, in the 11th and 12th of William III. This Act abolifhed all jurifdiction in that cafe, in the Courts in the Plantations. The SOLE power of trying fuch offences, in the Colonies, was vefted in Commiffioners, appointed under the Great Seal of England, or Seal of the Admiralty, according to the courfe of the Admiralty, that is to fay, WITHOUT JURY. The Commiffioners were alfo impowered to iſſue warrants, in any of the Colonies, for arrefting fuch Pirates or their acceffaries. They might, at difcretion, either try the criminals in America, or fend them to England to be tried. Should the Governors of any Charter or Proprietary Government refufe to aſſiſt the Commiffioners; fhould any perfon in authority, in the Colonies, refufe to pay obedience to the Act;

fuch

such refusal, in either case, was declared to be a forfeiture of the Charter.

An Act passed in the 10th and 11th year of the same reign, confines the advantage of the Fishery of Newfoundland to British ships fitted out from Great-Britain. The execution of the orders and regulations respecting that Fishery, was placed in the hands of the Admirals, in the respective harbours; that is to say, in the hands of the Master of the ship that should first arrive from Great-Britain. The decision in all questions of civil suit is vested in such Admirals, with appeal to the Commander of the King's ships. All criminal offences are to be tried, in any County of England, by the King's Commissioners of Oyer and Terminer and Goal delivery.

The opinions of this Nation concerning the Government of the Colonies, may be collected from the above Acts. The authority of Parliament to bind America, in all cases whatsoever, and whenever the general interest of the whole Empire required it, was never disputed; and it was often exerted to correct abuses, and to suppress the ideas of independence, which began, even then, to be cherished

cherished by the Colonies. The same principles and the same policy, were carried down by Parliament through the three succeeding reigns of Queen Anne, and of George I. and George II.

Early in the first of those reigns, the grossest abuses were committed by the petty Legislatures in the Colonies, with respect to Coin. The interposition of Parliament became necessary to correct those abuses. An Act was passed in the 6th of Queen Anne, for that purpose; when the Councils of that Princess were guided by Whigs. By this Act the rates of Foreign Coin, in the Plantations, were ascertained; and a severe punishment was inflicted on those who should take them at higher rates. The American Trade was placed in the same reign under further restrictions, by Act of Parliament. Rice and Molasses were added to the list of enumerated commodities. In the reign of George I. Furs and Copper-ore of the Plantations were subjected to the same restrictions.

The British Parliament confined not to Acts their sense of the undoubted right they possessed of controuling the Colonies, in all cases whatsoever. In the Journals of both Houses, there are many Proceedings which furnish proofs of their undeviating

viating adherence to the same principles. In the year 1702, a Bill was brought into the House of Commons, for abolishing all the Charter and Proprietary Governments in America, and reuniting them to the Crown. In 1705, the House of Lords came to several Resolutions on the subject of laws enacted in several of those Governments. They declared those laws to be repugnant to the laws of England, and destructive to the Constitution. This proceeding was likewise followed by a Bill for abolishing those Charters.

These Bills, it must be confessed, were not carried into laws. But they did not fail, through any doubt entertained by the Legislature against their propriety. They were lost through a change in the situation of those, who brought forward the measure. That the opinion of the Legislature continued the same on this subject, is evident; as the same proposition was again taken up in the year 1716; when a WHIG Ministry governed the Kingdom.

In the reign of George II. the instances of the controuling authority of Parliament over the Colonies, are more numerous and striking. By an Act of the 2d of George II. Chap. 35. severe prohibitions

hibitions and penalties are imposed and inflicted on such persons as shall cut and destroy white Pine-trees, tho' such Pines are growing within the limits of a Township already granted; and these penalties are directed to be sued for and recovered in the Courts of Admiralty. The Merchants of Great-Britain having, in the 5th of the same reign, preferred a Petition to Parliament, complaining of the difficulties they met with in the recovery of debts in the Plantations; an Act was passed, which subjected all real Estates in the Colonies to just debts and demands; and to be assets, in the same manner as in England, for the satisfaction of debts due by Bond. The exportation of Hats from any of the Colonies, and even the conveyance of them by land from one Colony to another, is prohibited, under severe penalties, by an Act passed in the same Session.

In the year 1733 the Province of Massachusett's-Bay presented a Petition to the House of Commons, praying that they might be heard by Counsel on the subject of Grievances. The chief of these was, " That the Crown had restrained their " Governour, by instructions, in certain cases re-" lative to the issue and disposal of Public Money, " and the emission of Paper-Bills of Credit." The Commons, having considered the matter, came to a

F   Resolution,

Refolution, "That the Petition was frivolous and
"groundlefs, a high infult upon his Majefty's Go-
"vernment, and tending to SHAKE OFF THE DE-
"PENDENCY of the faid Colony upon this King-
"dom, to which in LAW and RIGHT THEY OUGHT
"TO BE SUBJECT." Complaint having, at the
fame time, been made to the Houfe, "That the
"Reprefentatives of that Colony had CENSURED a
"perfon for giving evidence, before a Committee
"of the Houfe, in the cafe of a Bill then depend-
"ing in Parliament;" it was refolved, "That the
"paffing fuch cenfure was an AUDACIOUS PRO-
"CEEDING, and a high violation of the privi-
"leges of the Houfe." A Committee was accordingly appointed to enquire who were the
abettors of this unwarrantable proceeding.

We may perceive, from the above circumftance,
how jealous Parliament HAVE BEEN of their fupremacy and uncontroulable authority over the
Colonies. Another inftance muft carry the proof
of this pofition beyond the power of reply. In
the year 1740, the Houfe of Commons entered
into a confideration of "the abufes committed in
"the Colonies, in refpect to the emiffion of Paper
"Bills of Credit." After a long examination, they
came to various Refolutions. They refolved,
"That

" That the Act passed in the 6th of Queen Anne,
" ascertaining the rates of Foreign Coin in America,
" had not been duly observed. That many indi-
" rect practices, in that respect, had been introduced,
" contrary to the true intent of the Act. That an
" Address should be presented to his Majesty to
" require the Governors of his Colonies to take
" effectual measures for the strict observance of
" the Act of the 6th of Queen Anne. That
" another Address should be presented, request-
" ing his Majesty to issue his Royal Proclamation,
" to settle and ascertain the rates of Foreign Gold
" Coins. That the CREATING and issuing Bills of
" Credit, in the British Colonies, by virtue of Acts
" of Assembly, had frustrated the design of the
" Act of the 6th of Queen Anne. That an
" humble Address of Thanks should be presented
" to his Majesty, for the orders he has already
" given on that head; and, That he should also
" be requested to require and command the Go-
" vernors of the respective Provinces, not to give
" their assent to any Act, whereby Bills of Credit
" might be issued in lieu of Money."

These spirited Resolutions of the Commons checked, for some time, the abuses in the emission and circulation of Paper-Money. The New-England Governments, however, did not continue long to pay any regard to ROYAL Inſtructions, though ſupported and enforced by the authority of the Houſe of Commons. The frauds committed awakened again the attention of Parliament. In the 24th of George II. an Act was paſſed, " to " regulate and reſtrain Paper-bills of Credit in the " Four New-England Governments." The Governors of thoſe Colonies were prohibited, under pain of being removed from their Governments, and for ever rendered incapable of any public office or place of truſt, from aſſenting to any Act, Order, or Vote, for the iſſue of any Paper-bills of Credit; and all ſuch Acts, Orders, or Votes, were declared to be, *ipſo facto*, null and void.

In the year 1741 the Colonies took up the idea of a LAND-BANK, which had proved ſo unſucceſsful in England in the reign of King William. The "American Aſſemblies," it appeared to Parliament, " had PRESUMED to publiſh a ſcheme " for ſupplying a pretended want of a medium in " trade, for ſetting up a Bank on land ſecurity, " and to ſolicit ſubſcriptions." To correct this evil, an Act was paſſed, in the 14th of George II.

" to

" to restrain and prevent such unwarrantable prac-
" tices; and to extend to America, the penalties
" inflicted by a Statute of the 6th of George I. on
" persons guilty of such practices in these king-
" doms." They were also subjected, by the same
Act, to the penalty and forfeiture ordained by
the Statute of Provision and PREMUNIRE of the
16th of Richard the Second.

There are several other Statutes by which Parliament with equal force assert their authority over
the Colonies. In some of these, they carry this
authority beyond the limits, with which they have
hitherto circumscribed it in this Kingdom. In
the 29th of George II. cap. 35. Officers of the
Army are empowered to enlist, in the Colonies, ap-
prentices and indented servants. The persons so
enlisted were exempted from arrests in civil actions,
where the value of the action exceeds not ten
pounds. To these striking instances of the controuling power of Parliament over the Colonies,
may be added the Act of 23d of George II. cap. 29.
By that Act, " every person erecting or working
" any mill or other engine for slitting or rolling
" iron, or any plating forge or furnace for making
" steel, is subjected to a penalty of 200l. to be
" recovered in any of the Courts in Westminster-
                                            " Hall,

" Hall, or in the Court of Exchequer in Scot-
" land."

The foregoing recital of Statutes binding the Colonies, prior to the present reign, of which the Congress so much complain, is sufficient to convince the dispassionate, that the controuling power of Parliament has been perpetually exerted, and never disputed. There is hardly any object of Legiflation in which the laws of this Country have not bound America. The Congress, whilft they affect to disavow the supremacy of the British Legislature, acknowledge that supremacy, perhaps thro' inadvertence, in its utmost latitude. They own themselves the subjects of the King of Great-Britain, yet it was the British Legislature that placed his Majesty and his family on the Throne. Were the Colonies represented in the Parliament which limited the succession of the Crown to the House of Hanover, any more than they were in THAT which laid a paltry Duty on tea in the Ports of America? His Majesty owes his Throne to the Laws of England; and, as King, he can have no subject that is not bound by that law.

Taxation has been purposely omitted in the above detail. That article, as the great object of contest,
ought

ought to be separately stated. The several instances of the exercise of the power of Parliament, in that case, shall be, therefore, thrown into one Point of view. The first instance of Taxation is the Act of the 12th of Charles II. for granting to the Crown a duty of Tonnage and Poundage. This Act is in point. It directs, that the duties abovementioned " shall be payable upon commodities not only " imported into the realm of England, but also " into the DOMINIONS THEREUNTO BELONGING." The Colonies are here included in express words. It is true, indeed, that the Duties of Tonnage and Poundage were NOT collected in America. The reason was, that the commerce of the Plantations was so inconsiderable, that the revenue arising from it could not pay the expence of collection.

But whatever might have been the reason for NOT collecting the Duties of Tonnage and Poundage in the Colonies, the Law was certainly understood to extend to America. In the year 1680, the Assembly of the Island of Jamaica refused " to raise " levies for the support of Government." Upon this refusal, the Lords of the Council made a Minute " to confer with the Judges upon the question: " Whether the subsidies upon the Tonnage and " Poundage upon goods that may by Law,

or

" or shall be directly carried to Jamaica, be not
" payable, according to Law, by his Majesty's
" subjects inhabiting that Island, or trading there,
" by virtue of the Acts of Tonnage and Poundage,
" or other Acts made in England?" Unfortunately
it does not appear, whether the conference was ever
held; or if it was actually held, what was the result.

The 25th of Charles II. cap. 7. is the next
Act that binds America, in point of Taxation.
By that Act certain duties are made payable in the
Plantations, upon sugar, tobacco, cotton-wool,
indigo, ginger, logwood, fustic, and other dying
woods, and cocoa-nuts exported to any other place,
except England. These Duties continue to be
paid to this day.

In the 9th of Queen Anne, an Act was passed,
imposing certain Duties on all prize-goods taken
in America, and imported into any of the Colonies.
These Duties were as follows: " All European
" goods (wine and brandy excepted) which have
" been usually sent to the Plantations, are to pay
" THERE such Customs, as are payable for the
" like goods imported into the Plantations from
" Great-Britain. Other goods taken as prizes
" shall be liable THERE to such Duties as were
" payable

" payable for the fame, by any Act of Affembly,
" in the faid Plantations."

To thefe Acts, fubjecting his Majefty's fubjects in America to Taxes impofed by the Britifh Parliament, feveral others may be added. The Act of the 9th of Queen Anne, for eftablifhing a Poft-office. The various Acts paffed for levying and inforcing the collection of the duty of fixpence per month, out of Seamen's wages, for the fupport of Greenwich Hofpital. All thefe Acts extend to America. They bind the Colonies, as well as the Mother-Country. Their authority was never difputed; and the Taxes impofed by them have been uniformly raifed. The Act of the 2d of George II. cap. 7. is ftill more explicit and decifive in the words. It requires the payment of the Duties for Greenwich Hofpital, " by
" feamen belonging to American fhips, whether
" employed upon the high feas, or in any port,
" harbour, bay or creek, within ANY of the Co-
" lonies."

It appears from this detail of facts, that the right of Parliament to bind the Colonies, in all cafes whatfoever, is not a claim founded on mere theory: on the contrary, that the controuling power

power of the Legiflature is warranted by conftant ufage, and uninterrupted practice. That the Declaratory Act, of which the Americans complain, contains no new, no affumed powers over the Plantations; and that there is fcarce any channel of Legiflation, through which the Britifh Parliament has NOT exerted its fupremacy, in as full and ample a manner as it has been exerted over the inhabitants of Great-Britain; and all this prior to the prefent reign, in which the Congrefs place the commencement of " Public Ruin."

The American Congrefs, with a partiality for themfelves fcarcely confiftent with their defign of gaining others, in the next paragraph of their Declaration, call the Acts, which were the CONSEQUENCE of the refiftance of their conftituents, the CAUSE of their rebellion. In defcending to particulars, their firft complaint is ftated againft " the ex-
" tenfion of the jurifdiction of the Courts of Admi-
" ralty and Vice-Admiralty beyond their former
" limits;" by which, they alledge, " the fubject
" is deprived of his inherent right of a trial by
" Jury." The Congrefs furely forget, or it is not confiftent with their defign to remember, that the alterations of which they complain were made at the requeft of their conftituents. The reafons

fons affigned for this requeft were, that the Courts of Admiralty eftablifhed formerly in the various Provinces, poffeffed fo little dignity, on account of the dependence and poverty of the judges, that juftice was either facrificed to connexions, or biaffed by avarice. Befides that, Appeals to Great-Britain could be feldom made, on account of the expence and diftance. To remedy this evil, the prefent eftablifhment of Courts of Admiralty in America was formed. Four great Courts of Vice-Admiralty were erected. The Judges were rendered independent by ample falaries. The line of Appeal became fhort, eafy, and obvious; and as to trial by Jury, the whole world knows that the Court of Admiralty in England never admitted that mode of trial in civil cafes.

The complaint of the Congrefs, with regard to the Bill for fhutting the Port of Bofton, is ridiculous as well as unjuft, as the inhabitants of that place had it in their own power to remove the grievance. The deftruction of the Eaft-India Company's tea, at Bofton, is well known to have been the deliberate act of a very great majority of the inhabitants. To obtain reparation by the common courfe of law was impoffible, where the number of the offenders fcreened them effectually

ally from juftice. It was a public crime, and the punifhment ought to have been general. In purfuance of that plan of tendernefs, which has been fatally loft on the Americans, the Bill for fufpending the trade of Bofton was rendered conditional. A door was left open for an immediate reconciliation, fhould the Affembly of Maffachufett's-Bay make a public grant, for repairing the damage fuftained, by a Company of Merchants, through a public outrage. Yet the Congrefs ftigmatize with the name of injuftice, a coercive ftatute rendered abfolutely neceffary by the fhamelefs depredations of the inhabitants of Bofton; and which ftatute, they themfelves had it in their power to terminate, in an inftant, by doing an act of common juftice.

But why fhould we expect common juftice towards others, among a people, who (with regard to the Tea-Act) have been manifeftly unjuft to themfelves? It is of the Duty on Tea, the Americans principally complain; yet they fubmitted to a Duty of 7 l. per Ton, laid on Wines, the Seffion which immediately preceded the paffing of the Tea-Act. The Duty on Tea was alfo fubmitted to in all the Provinces where that commodity had not been ufually introduced by Smuggling. Bofton itfelf, self, and even Mr. John Hancock (now PRESIDENT of the Congress, but formerly a most notorious SMUGGLER), originally made no objection to the Act. It was when the East-India Company, by adopting the plan of sending Tea to America in their own name, gave the finishing blow to Smuggling, that the inhabitants of Massachusett's-Bay determined to oppose the Duty. Prior to the Act for laying the THREE-PENCE Duty on Tea, payable in the Colonies, the Americans actually paid a SHILLING, together with the profit of the Merchant. Formerly all Tea exported to the Plantations went encumbered with a Shilling, paid by the East-India Company. In other words, the Duty was not drawn back on exportation; so that, by the Act, the consumer is a gainer of a Shilling in every pound of Tea, if to the nine-pence duty we should add commission, insurance, freight, and profit. Smugglers found themselves incapable of carrying on their contraband commerce; and they inflamed an ignorant rabble, to serve their own interest, or to gratify their own revenge.

With equal effrontery, and with still less reason, the Congress exclaim against the alteration made in the form of the government of Boston. With their usual fallacy in argument, the Americans wish to establish

establish it as a maxim in polity, That Charters granted by the CROWN, can neither be reversed or altered by the LEGISLATURE. They might as well go at once to the whole supremacy; and save themselves the trouble of thus supporting a cause untenable on any other grounds. The three branches of the Legislature united make daily alterations in the Constitution of Great Britain; and, if their Supremacy extends over the whole empire, they have the same right to alter the constitution of the American Colonies. If the Americans deny this position, all argument is at an end; and they avow an independence, which, in THEIR circumstances, marks them out for enemies. After all, this alteration of which the Congress affect to complain, is no more than putting the inhabitants of Massachuset's-Bay on the same footing with the other Colonies. They have received in miniature the counter-part of the constitution of the Mother-Kingdom; and have THEY a right, or can THEY wish to be more free than the freest nation in the world?

The Act for regulating the Government of Quebec, furnishes the Congress with an ample field for declamation. To inveigh against Popery and Arbitrary Power has been ever a favourite

vourite topic with men, who wish to profit by the prejudices of the people. Had the Congress attended to the general principles of the British Constitution, they might have informed themselves, that His Majesty, without the interposition of the two other branches of the Legislature, might have permitted the inhabitants of Canada to remain for ever under French laws. There is no maxim in the Law of England more generally known or less controverted than, That in conquered or ceded countries, which have already laws of their own, such laws remain in full force, till they are altered and changed by the Sovereign. Had His Majesty, therefore, entertained such designs, as the Congress obliquely lay to his charge, why should he call in the aid of the Legislature to execute what was already done by the Common Law? The Congress will not, surely, affirm, that the system of government established by the Legislature in Quebec, is so arbitrary in itself, or so fit for the purposes of despotism, as the Constitution which subsisted in that Province under the French. Ought they not to consider, that no other form of government could have been established, so suitable to the disposition of the inhabitants, the tenures of their property, and the toleration of

their

their religion, to all which they had an undoubted right, by the terms of their Capitulation and the articles of the fubfequent Treaty of Peace?

The Oppofition at HOME, as well as the Patriots ABROAD, have found an extenfive fubject for pathetic eloquence, in the form of Government now eftablifhed by Law in Canada. The FORMER have either very treacherous memories, or they change without any ceremony their opinions with their fituation. Under the adminiftration of the EARL of CHATHAM, Mr. Morgan, Lord SHELBURNE's Secretary, was fent PRIVATELY to America, as Commiffioner, to fettle and regulate a new code for the Government of Quebec. The Governor and Chief Juftice of that Province, if I am not miftaken, were joined with Morgan in this SECRET, but important commiffion. The meafure, it is faid, was confidered by the Board of Trade; it was certainly debated, if not adopted by the Cabinet, as far back as the year 1767, during the plenitude of the Earl of Chatham's power. Lord Camden was Chancellor, and gave his fanction to regulations MORE ALLIED TO DESPOTISM than thofe he reprobates at prefent. The Duke of Grafton, the Earl of Shelburne, General Conway, and feveral others of " that illuftrious Band," on whofe virtues the Americans

ricans expatiate with rapture, approved this POPISH, ARBITRARY, TYRANNICAL system of Government*: yet all thefe are, now, true Americans, ſtrenuous Proteſtants, Whigs of the ancient mould, determined aſſertors of public freedom, avowed enemies to OPPRESSION, POPERY, and ARBITRARY POWER!

The Congreſs enumerate, among their complaints againſt the Britiſh Legiſlature, the Reſolution of Parliament to give its due force to an unrepealed ſtatute paſſed in the time of Henry VIII. It is declared in the Reſolution, that upon this ſtatute, treaſons and miſpriſions of treaſon committed in any of his Majeſty's dominions beyond ſea, ſubject to the Crown of Great-Britain, may be tried in England. Though this Reſolution is conſidered by the Congreſs as a part of the ideal ſyſtem of enſlavement, with which they charge the King and Parliament, it contains no novelty, no uncommon ſtretch of law. A thouſand inſtances of the ſame kind are upon record, long before the preſent diſputes with America began. One inſtance is extremely remarkable; I mean, the tranſactions in the Caſe of the Inſurrection in

---

* Lord Rockingham had the *merit* of ſending a *Popiſh* Biſhop to Quebec.

Antigua,

Antigua, in the year 1711. All the proceedings were founded on the Act of Henry VIII. Some of the Insurgents were sent to England; they were tried upon that Statute; and that circumstance has established a precedent which cannot be controverted. But had even a new law of this kind been made, what reason could the American Congress have to complain? Have not the prejudices, insurrections, and even rebellion of their own countrymen totally interrupted the common course of justice over all the vast Continent which they inhabit; and shall the generality of the crime be admitted a competent excuse against punishment?

From condemning the Acts of the Legislature, the Congress pass to complaints against their Sovereign, as well as his principal servants. They alledge, that the " Americans have incessantly " and ineffectually besieged the Throne for ten " years;" yet conceal the reason, which was, That their demands, rather than requests, were such as the Sovereign could not grant, consistent with the powers vested in him by the Constitution. They complain, that fleets and armies have been sent to their country, to enforce the coercive laws enacted by the Legislature, for the establishment of its supremacy; yet they pass over in silence the outrages committed by themselves, which

which rendered that meafure neceffary. Did they not draw the fword with one hand, when the other was ftretched forth with petitions for relief from pretended grievances? Did they not purchafe arms, ammunition, and artillery, form magazines, enlift foldiers, and prepare, in every refpect, for rebellion and war, when they affected to fpeak the language of fubmiffion and peace?

All thefe are facts that cannot be controverted. The Congrefs know the truth, but purfue their plan of deception. "They hoped in vain," they fay, "for moderation in their enemies;" yet their own conduct has been one continued feries of violence, oppreffion, and injuftice. Having difclaimed their allegiance to the Sovereign, difobeyed the acts of the Legiflature, deftroyed the property, and infulted the perfons of the fervants of the State, affumed the functions of fovereignty, and rufhed into actual rebellion; they complain of a want of moderation in Government, for exerting the power vefted in it by the Conftitution, for reftoring tranquillity, enforcing legal fubmiffion to the laws of the State, and for protecting the injured and punifhing the guilty.

Throughout the whole of their ftrange Declaration, the American Congrefs appear to adapt

their reasonings to the weakness of the prejudiced, and their facts to the credulity of the ignorant. They affirm, that they have uniformly endeavoured to procure an accommodation with the Mother-Country; yet they reprobate the Resolution of the Commons, on the 20th of February, which opened a fair channel for agreement. They call the Resolution " an insidious manœuvre, cal-
" culated to divide the Americans, and to esta-
" blish a perpetual auction of taxation, where
" Colony should bid against Colony, all of them
" uninformed what ransom should redeem their
" lives; and thus to extort from them, at the
" point of the bayonet, the unknown sums that
" should be sufficient to gratify, if possible to
" gratify ministerial rapacity, with the miserable
" indulgence left them of raising, in their own
" mode, the prescribed tribute." We may learn, from this tedious and involved sentence, how much the Congress have profited by the speeches of Patriotism in the British Parliament. A noted Orator, who has been suspected of having penned the DECLARATORY BILL, (which, the Congress alledge, contains the whole mass of American grievances) used almost the same words in the House of Commons, on the day the Resolution came under debate. But former demerits have been forgot, in what the American Demagogues foolishly construe into present services.

To shew the nature of the Proposition which the Congress stigmatize with the name of an "in-"sidious manœuvre," some previous facts must be explained. On the second of February, a Motion was made in the House of Commons, for an Address to his Majesty, which was soon after presented, with the concurrence of the Lords. In this Address, the two Houses having stated some facts, were induced to declare, that a rebellion actually existed at that time in the Province of Massachuset's-bay: That this conduct was the more inexcusable, when it was considered with how much temper his Majesty and the two Houses of Parliament had acted, in support of the Laws and Constitution of Great-Britain : That they were resolved never so far to desert the trust reposed in them, as to relinquish ANY PART *of the* SOVEREIGN AUTHORITY *over* ALL *his* MAJESTY'S DOMINIONS, which the law invested in his Majesty and the two Houses of Parliament: That the conduct of the Americans was sufficient to convince them of the necessity of this supremacy and power: That, however, they had always been, and always should be ready to pay attention and regard to any real grievances, which should be laid before them in a DUTIFUL and CONSTITUTIONAL manner: That they requested his Majesty to take the most effectual measures to enforce due obedience to the laws

laws and authority of the Supreme Legiflature: And that they were refolved, at the hazard of their lives and fortunes, to fupport his Majefty againft all rebellious attempts, in the maintenance of the juft rights of his Majefty and the two Houfes of Parliament.

In this Addrefs the two Houfes of Parliament, while they held forth the Sword in one hand, evidently tendered the Olive-branch with the other. The Americans themfelves were made the arbiters of their own fate. The choice of war or peace was left in their own hands. But as the offer of Parliament to liften to the real grievances of the Colonifts was deemed too general to form a foundation for an agreement between them and the Mother-country, the Minifter, wifhing to conciliate matters with America, even contrary to the opinion of many Friends to this Country, laid before the Houfe of Commons fome EXPLICIT PROPOSITIONS, which might anfwer that end. Accordingly, on the twentieth of February, the following Propofitions were introduced to a Committee of the whole Houfe, by the Chancellor of the Exchequer: " That it is the opinion of this
" Committee, that when the Governor, Council,
" and Affembly, or General Court of his Majefty's
" Provinces or Colonies fhall propofe to make pro-
" vifion

"vision according to their respective conditions,
"circumstances, and situations, for contributing
"their proportion to the common defence; such
"proportion to be raised under the authorities of
"the General Court, or General Assembly of such
"Province or Colony, and disposable by Parlia-
"ment; and shall engage to make provision also
"for the support of the Civil Government, and
"the administration of justice in such Province
"or Colony; it will be proper, if such proposal
"shall be approved by his Majesty in Parliament,
"and for so long as such provision shall be made
"accordingly, to forbear in respect of such Pro-
"vince, or Colony, to levy any duties, tax, or
"assessment, or to impose any further duty, tax,
"or assessment, except only such duties as it may
"be expedient to impose for the regulation of
"Commerce; the nett produce of the duties last
"mentioned, to be carried to the account of such
"Province, Colony, or Plantation respectively."

This Resolution, which was carried by a great majority, plainly marked the ground for a negotiation, and an equitable agreement with the Colonies. It was moderate, comprehensive, and explicit. It named the persons from whom the proposals must come, and those to whom they were to be made. The end and purpose of the Contribution were explained. The appropriation of the expected revenue was specified, and precluded every suspicion of its being misapplied. Though the offer was conditional, it was plainly conclusive, as long as the Americans themselves should adhere to the agreement. They had it in their power to tax themselves, the great point for which they professed to contend; and the only right reserved by the Legislature was, to determine the QUANTUM of the supply; and they alone can determine it, as being the supreme power, who are the sole judges of what is necessary to support the State. The Proposition, upon the whole, was AT LEAST as favourable to the pretensions of the Americans, as to the claims of the Mother-Country. The former, therefore, must have accepted the proposal, had what they held forth to the Public formed the real principles of their opposition.

The Minority in Parliament, who deemed nothing so fatal to their own views, as an agreement with the Americans, upon equitable, and consequently permanent terms, opposed this Proposition as insidious in its nature, and for that purpose rendered obscure and perplexed in its language. The American Demagogues, whose influence can only exist in the midst of anarchy and confusion, opposed it with similar views. The latter,

latter, indeed, have approved fo much of the SENTIMENTS, or rather PROFESSIONS of the former, that they have, in their Declaration, echoed back their very words in Parliament. The argument before went only to the claim of the Americans to be permitted, in their Affemblies, to fettle the mode of Taxation. They then demanded an exclufive privilege of fixing the amount or quantum of the fupply; and now they will give no fupply at all. But if neither the mode nor the QUANTUM is to be left in the power of Parliament, what power has Parliament left, with regard to the taxing of the Americans? Ought the BRITISH LEGISLATURE to lay HUMBLY the wants of the Public before the PETTY LEGISLATURES of America, and requeft *their* aid for the general fupport of Government? What would this be, but the total emancipation of the Colonies from that fupremacy for which we contend?

The Americans, formerly, declared themfelves willing to contribute to the exigences and expences of the State, provided the demand fhould come by requifition from the King, and not by an immediate exertion of Parliamentary authority. This offer his Majefty declined, with that patriotifm which has uniformly marked his OWN meafures,

during

during his reign. Anxious for the happiness of ALL his subjects, he chose to be the Monarch of ONE great and free nation, rather than the Sovereign of a number of petty States, weakened by their own disunion. Had his Majesty been actuated by those motives of ambition, which are not uncommon among Princes, he would have eagerly closed with the offers of the Americans. Instead of making himself dependent, for the maintenance of his dignity, upon the grants of ONE Assembly, he might have extricated himself from even the fear of pecuniary difficulties, by a proper management of many Assemblies. The Representatives of one Province might be gratified into the views of the Crown, from the revenue of another; British Members might receive the wages of corruption in America; and American Representatives be sent for the price of their votes to this Kingdom.

But succeeding events have demonstrated, that the Americans were not sincere, in any one of their declarations, in favour of an amicable accommodation. The Propositions voted, on the 20th of February, came up to their own former demands; yet they evaded them, by treating them as insidious. The truth is, they knew their own demerits towards this Country, and they could not believe,

that

that proposals so highly favourable could have been, on her part, sincere. One good, however, has resulted from the Propositions. The Colonies, by rejecting them, have left no doubt remaining concerning their real intentions. They confine no longer their claims to the exclusive privilege of taxing themselves. They aim, evidently, at a total independence in all matters whatsoever; and more particularly with regard to the Act of Navigation. They have long made secret but most dangerous encroachments on this PALLADIUM of our Commerce. They now publickly avow their resolution to pay no regard to any Parliamentary restrictions, whether ancient or recent, on THEIR Commerce. They now openly trade all over Europe; and the obtaining the privilege, which they have, at length, usurped, has been the primary cause of their resistance to Parliament. The manufacturers and merchants of this Country have been long no strangers to this American policy; yet the Congress have the effrontery to expect, that the mercantile interest of Great Britain will espouse their cause.

The American Congress, having in a loose, cursory, and superficial manner, advanced some pretended arguments to justify their rebellion, descend

descend to the misrepresentation of facts, with the same design. They affirm, " That General Gage, " who had occupied Boston as a garrison, sent out " a large detachment of his army, on the 19th " of April, who made an unprovoked assault on " the inhabitants of the Province of Boston, at " Lexington." On this allegation of the Congress, it may be remarked, that the rebellious conduct of the Town of Boston, where all the authority of legal government had been long extinguished by the tyranny of a rabble instigated by factious leaders, had rendered a force necessary in that place, to restore order and tranquillity, to protect the innocent, and to restrain the excesses of the turbulent and guilty. That the military preparations made in all parts of the Province, and especially at the Town of Concord, with the avowed intention of opposing all legal authority, induced and even forced General Gage (though fatally too late) to send out a detachment of the troops under his command, to prevent hostilities, by seizing the means of carrying them on. That some of the Inhabitants of the Province, in " war- " like array," stood in the way of this detachment, with arms in their hands; and that when ordered to remove in a peaceable manner, they made " an unprovoked assault" on his Majesty's troops,

troops, by firing FIRST upon them, and killing some, and wounding many.

The audacity of the Congress, in asserting FALSEHOODS, demands a brief detail of the TRUTH. General Gage, having been informed that arms, ammunition, cannon, and other implements of war, had been collected in the town of Concord, ordered a detachment of the Army to march with all possible secrecy to that place. He gave orders to the detachment, to observe the most strict discipline, and to resent no insults offered them by the country people, except actual hostilities. The General's orders were, in truth, too implicitly observed. There was not one LOADED MUSQUET in the whole detachment, except those in the hands of FIFTY Marines, who formed the van, when they were FIRED upon, by the country people, at Lexington. The affidavits of the rebels, on this subject, are impositions and perjuries. There is not a man, whether officer or soldier, in the whole detachment, consisting of 800 men, but is ready, in the most solemn manner, to attest the truth of this fact.

It were to be wished, for the honour of the insurgents, that their BARBAROUS CRUELTY to

the

the wounded soldiers, were more problematical than their firing FIRST on the King's troops. The soldiers who fell by the first fire of the rebels, were found scalped, when the detachment returned from Concord to Lexington Bridge. Two soldiers who lay wounded on the field, and had been scalped by the savage Provincials, were still breathing. They appeared, by the traces of blood, to have rolled in the agonies of this horrid species of death, several yards from the place where they had been scalped. Near these unfortunate men, another dreadful object presented itself. A soldier who had been slightly wounded, appeared with his eyes torn out of their sockets, by the barbarous mode of GOOGING, a word and practice peculiar to the Americans. Humanity forbids us to dwell longer on this scene of horror. The rebels, to break the force of accusation, began to recriminate. They laid several instances of wanton cruelty to the charge of the troops; yet nothing is better ascertained, than that not one of the soldiers ever quitted the road, either upon their march or return from Concord.

The Congress stigmatize the expedition to Lexington and Concord, with the epithets " of an un-" provoked and wanton assault." Was the collecting

lecting warlike implements at Concord, raising men throughout the Province, disciplining troops in every district, forming magazines, purchasing ammunition, and preparing arms, no provocation? Were not the whole Country assembled before they knew of this expedition? And was not their being so completely provided with the means of repelling hostilities, a sufficient proof, that they had previously resolved to commence them? Could TEN THOUSAND men, the number that attacked (though at a PRUDENT distance) the troops on their retreat, have been collected by accident, or called together by a sudden alarm? Are not the Congress conscious to themselves, and was not General Gage sufficiently apprized, that the people of Massachusets-Bay had determined to begin hostilities, had the expedition to Concord never happened? The truth is, the march of the troops had only hastened the execution of the plan of rebellion settled before in the secret Councils of the Provincial Congress.

The assertions of the Congress concerning transactions within the town of Boston, are as utterly devoid of truth, as their account of what happened in the country. The hostile intentions of those WITHIN, were as apparent as the rebellion of of their brethren WITHOUT was certain. The great law of self-defence must therefore have justified General Gage for having deprived the former of arms, which they almost avowedly intended to raise against all legal authority. After the skirmish at Lexington and Concord, all supplies from the country were cut off from the town of Boston. Many of the inhabitants desired to remove, with their effects. Their request was granted; but it was at the same time demanded, that they should deliver up their arms. This was, at first, approved by all; but great clamours soon after followed. Such of the inhabitants as were well affected, or pretended to be well affected to Government, alledged, that none but the ill-inclined shewed any inclination to remove; and that when they should become safe with their effects, the town would be set on fire. A great demur having also arisen about the meaning of the word EFFECTS, whether MERCHANDISE was included; and the General being likewise sensible, that the permitting articles of that kind to be carried to the rebels, might strengthen them in their resistance; he retained the goods. But they are still safely kept for the owners, should they either continue faithful, or seize his Majesty's mercy, and return to their duty.

The

The next paragraph of the Declaration, as it is not supported by truth, is addressed to the passions. The Congress complain, with an attempt at the pathos, " of the separation of wives from " their husbands, children from their parents, and " the aged and sick from their relations and " friends." But is it not notorious to the whole world, that this SEPARATION, which the Congress affect to lament, was the necessary consequence of the rebellion of their countrymen? Did they not surround the town of Boston, with an armed force, with the avowed intention of destroying his Majesty's forces, Generals, and Governor? And were the gates to be left open " to let ruin " enter," as one of their own writers expresses himself? Have the people of Boston suffered more hardships than the inhabitants of besieged towns usually suffer? Have they not even suffered fewer restraints than men in their situation had reason to expect? Was not Dr. Warren, the Chairman of the Provincial Congress, a notorious abettor of the insurrection, a nominal General in a rebel army, permitted to come into Boston, under pretence of visiting a sick friend, on the day preceding the action on Bunker's-hill, where he was killed in arms against his King and Country? Is this a mark of those cruel restraints, those melancholy

K separations,

separations, of which the Congress complain? But THEIR business is to engage the passions, where they can make no impression with their arguments.

In the next paragraph of their Declaration, the Congress, with their usual want of impartiality and fairness, mention the CONSEQUENCES of their own rebellion, as the cause of their taking up arms. They observe, that General Gage issued a Proclamation, "declaring all the inhabitants of "Massachusets-Bay rebels, suspending the course "of the Common Law, and publishing instead "thereof the use and exercise of the Law Martial."* But, did he declare them rebels till they had attacked his Majesty's troops, seized his forts and garrisons, besieged his army in the capital of the Province, and not only interrupted the common course of justice, but even totally annihilated all legal authority? It is with peculiar effrontery, that the Congress number the suspension of the common course of justice among their grievances, after all law and order had been trodden under foot by their own countrymen.

---

* This he was authorised to do, as civil Governor, by a Law passed in the Province, many years ago.

With the same degree of arrogant folly the Congress complain, that " their countrymen were " killed on Bunker's-hill, that Charles-town was " burnt to the ground, that their ships and vessels " have been seized, that their supplies of provi-" sions have been intercepted, that General Carle-" ton is instigating the Canadians and Indians " against them, and that domestic enemies are en-" couraged to attack them." All these things may certainly have happened; but have they not happened in consequence of their own rebellion? Have *they* a right to attack others, and have others no right to defend themselves? Do the inhabitants of Massachusets-Bay think, that as they have broken through all the ties that bind the subject to the Sovereign, the law of nature and of nations ought also to be suspended to gratify *their* ambition, to flatter *their* folly, to favour *their* extravagant schemes of independence? To the above imaginary catalogue of American grievances, may be opposed the just complaints of Great-Britain. Have not the rebels carried their hostilities to every corner against the Parent-State, that first gave them existence, and reared them to prosperity? Have they not attacked her troops at Lexington and at Concord, fired upon Boston, burnt the Light-house, taken Ticonderago and

Crown

Crown Point, and even penetrated into Canada? And have they not uſed every artifice to inſtigate the Savages to make war on their Sovereign and Mother-Country? Almoſt all theſe injuries preceded the juſt exertions of this Kingdom to puniſh their rebellion.

The concluſion of the Declaration, though laboured, contains nothing but empty declamation, and therefore merits little notice. The ſame diſregard to truth, or rather the ſame attention to miſrepreſentation, which diſtinguiſhes the reſt of that ſtrange compoſition, is carried down to the end. They alledge, " that they are reduced to the al-" ternative of chuſing an UNCONDITIONAL ſub-" miſſion to tyranny, or reſiſtance by force." The Congreſs ſurely forget, or it ſuits THEIR purpoſe to paſs over in ſilence, the favourable (perhaps too favourable) conditions offered to them, by the Reſolution of the Commons, in the month of February laſt. The terms couched in that Reſolution were ſo obviouſly advantageous to America, that the Oppoſition in Parliament declared them INSIDIOUS; or, in other words, " too good to be " ſincere." An amicable ſettlement had ceaſed to have been an object with the Demagogues ABROAD ; and it would have ruined the ſchemes of the Faction at home. The FORMER derived their influence, consequence, and power, from anarchy and confusion. THEY could exist only in a storm. The restoration of peace and tranquility must have reduced THEM to their original insignificance; and as for the LATTER, rendered desperate by disappointed ambition, they would not hesitate to ruin their Country, to procure the fall of their rivals.

Such being the state of opinions among the leaders of Faction on both sides of the Atlantic, "resistance by force became naturally the choice "of the Congress." To deceive an unhappy people, over whose minds they had established a temporary dominion, they boast of " their perfect union, " and their great INTERNAL resources; and that " foreign assistance is attainable." As to the first, we have no reason to give it implicit credit. The shew of unanimity, which now subsists in America, appears, from undoubted information, to be the effect of fear, more than any love for the desperate cause of the rebels. Men of property are, from interest, enemies to confusion; and the intelligent, foreseeing the inevitable issue of hostilities against the invincible power of a mighty Empire, are averse to a contest, that, on the side of the
Americans,

Americans, must terminate in ruin. But BOTH are terrified into silence by the tyranny of a misled rabble; or their STILL VOICE is drowned in the clamours of Faction and tumult of Party.

The INTERNAL RESOURCES of the Americans are as problematical, as their unanimity in rebellion. Consist these mighty resources in a wretched Paper-currency*, established on no ostensible fund of credit; and voted by an illegal Assembly, whose authority is feeble, on account of its novelty, and transitory, as it arises from temporary prejudices? Should force, or even folly, stamp a domestic value on the *paste-board* dollars of the Congress,

---

* These PAPER-RESOURCES have been very liberally exerted by the Colonists, in the course of the year 1775. Besides the sums voted by the General Congress, the Provincial Congresses have granted large subsidies, for supporting their respective opposition to Great-Britain. By the most authentic accounts, the following Colonies have raised the sums annexed to each.

	Currency.		Sterling.
Georgia		£.	10,000
South Carolina,	£. 1,000,000	or	150,000
North Carolina	50,000	or	30,000
Virginia	350,000	or	280,000
Maryland	100,000		
Rhode-Island	100,000	or	75,000

I have not been able to obtain any authentic Intelligence concerning the sums raised in the other Colonies. I may venture, however, to affirm, that the rebellious Provinces have raised, in the course of this year, a sum equal to the amount of their whole taxes (Provincial as well as Parliamentary) in SEVEN YEARS.

what

what foreign nation will receive them for its manufactures and commodities? Are the Americans themselves capable of furnishing all the great implements necessary for the prosecution of war? Can they supply their armies with tents, with powder, with cannon, or with musquets? Is any one of these articles manufactured in a sufficient quantity in America? And how can they be procured in Europe, with the wretched currency of the General Congress?

The Colonists, had not reason been warped by prejudice in every part of their conduct, might have foreseen, that their commencing a war deprived them instantly of the resources for carrying it on. Their whole Coast is lined, it is to be hoped, at this very moment, with our ships of war, to put a total stop to their Commerce. They have, therefore, lost at one stroke their whole trade in Corn and Rice with Spain, Portugal, and the Mediterranean; which, at a moderate computation, brought annually One Million Five Hundred Thousand Pounds to North America. They have lost the supplying our own West-India Islands, as well as those of other nations, with provisions; a branch of Commerce estimated little short of a Million annually. They have lost their

Fishery,

Fishery, an article too great for computation; and they have lost the exportation to Great-Britain of commodities which would not have answered in any other market, had the sea remained open to their Navigation.

But if the Americans have little reason to depend on DOMESTIC RESOURCES, they have still less to hope from FOREIGN AID. Will France, in the present state of her finances, involve herself in a ruinous and expensive war, to gratify the revenge of a Faction in this Country, or to favour the ambition of Demagogues beyond the Atlantic? Will Spain give her assistance to raise an INDEPENDENT EMPIRE in America? Will she encourage her own American subjects to rise against her authority, by abetting the rebellion of the American subjects of Great-Britain? Can either Branch of the House of Bourbon be so blind to its own interest, as to wish to see a Sovereign State erected so near its settlements, which, from their proximity, their produce, and their wealth, must, in such a case, become objects of invasion, depredation, and conquest? What has either France or Spain to fear from THIS KINGDOM, whose interest consists solely in preserving what she has already acquired? But have not BOTH every thing to fear, should a

new

new Sovereignty ſtart up in America, in which a want of reſources would, in ſome degree, juſtify the providing itſelf at the expence of wealthy neighbours?

Having endeavoured to terrify Great-Britain with their DOMESTIC reſources and FOREIGN aids; the Congreſs thinking, perhaps, they had gone too far, conclude with aſſurances, that " they have " not YET determined to diſſolve their union with " the Mother-Country." But that UNION, it appears from the ſequel, muſt not be conſtrued into SUBORDINATION, on the part of the Americans. The general ſupremacy of the Legiſlature, which by pervading the whole Britiſh Empire renders it ONE State, muſt not, it ſeems, croſs the Atlantic, but in ſuch proportions as may ſuit the inclinations of the Congreſs, " THEY have taken " up arms," as they openly avow, " againſt that " Supremacy;" and "THEY will not lay them down " till hoſtilities ſhall ceaſe on the part of Great- " Britain." This is the Ultimatum offered by the Congreſs: Withdraw your armies, recal your fleets, and you may have peace from the Americans; for, as " they fight not for conqueſt," they do not YET mean to transfer hoſtilities into the heart of theſe kingdoms!

The haughty Monarch who dreamt of univerſal monarchy in the laſt century, could ſcarcely have expreſſed himſelf in more inſolent terms to the petty Princes ſurrounding his dominions, than the Congreſs have done to the powerful Empire to which they owe the allegiance of ſubjects. Some allowance ought to be made for THEIR ignorance, and a great deal for the petulance of men new to conſequence and authority; but, even in that caſe, the inſolence of the Declaration is calculated to raiſe indignation, as well as contempt. The Congreſs, however, are only the echoes of a deſperate Faction in this Kingdom, who have uniformly, in their public exhibitions, degraded the ſtrength, power, and authority of Great-Britain, to exalt America on the ruins. With an effrontery without example in any other age or nation, THESE MEN aſſume the name of Patriots, yet lay the honour, dignity, and reputation of their Country under the feet of her rebellious ſubjects. With a peculiar refinement on Parricide, they bind the hands of the MOTHER, while they plant a dagger in thoſe of the DAUGHTER, to ſtab her to the heart; and, to finiſh the horrid picture, they ſmile at the miſchief they have done, and look round to the ſpectators for applauſe.

It appears, upon the whole, that the Declaration, which ought to contain all the argument in favour of the Americans, contains, in fact, nothing that does not militate against their cause. The right of taxing all the subjects of the Empire, for the general support of the State, is a part of that Supremacy which the first principles of the Constitution have vested in the British Legislature. This Supremacy has been exerted by Parliament, and admitted by the Americans, ever since their ancestors migrated from these kingdoms. If they now deny it, by that very act they cease to be subjects, and become rebels. But granting, for the sake of argument, that Taxation is no part of the supremacy of Parliament, the very conduct of the Americans not only justifies, but even renders it absolutely necessary, that a precedent should be made. They own, " that their internal " resources are great." The inability of contributing to the necessities of a State, from whom they have derived their origin, their support, their protection, and their prosperity, is no longer a pretence; and if they will give no Revenue as subjects, they owe a debt as allies. They affect to maintain armies by land. They threaten to send fleets to sea. They alledge, that their resources are capable of supporting a rebellion against the Mo-

her-

[76]

ther-Country; yet they juftify that rebellion by the demand made by the Mother-Country, for their bearing a part of their own FUTURE EXPENCES.

That the FORMER expences of America have drawn from Great-Britain an incredible treafure, may be feen from the following authentic eftimate. We fhall begin this eftimate with the acceffion of the Houfe of Hanover to the Throne of thefe Kingdoms.

	£.	s.	d.
From the year 1714 to the year 1775, the money voted by Parliament, for the forces employed in defence of the Colonies, amounts to	8,779,925	3	11½
Grants in Parliament, for rewards, encouragement, and indemnification to the Americans, during the laft war	1,081,771	11	9¼
Bounties on American commodities to the end of 1774	1,609,345	3	9¼
Sums granted to the Colonies, for the fupport of their Civil Government and Provincial Forces	3,835,900	7	4¼
Extraordinary expences for forts, garrifons, ordnance ftores, tranfports, carriages, provifions, may be eftimated equal to the expences of the forces	8,779,925	3	11½
Expences of fleets and naval ftations employed and eftablifhed in America for its defence may be eftimated at	10,000,000	00	00
Annual prefents to the American Indians, for abftaining from hoftilities againft the Colonies, and for the ceffion of lands,	610,000	00	00
	34,697,142	10	10¾

To

To this amazing sum might be added, by implication, the other expences of the two last Wars. The FORMER of those wars was undertaken for the protection of the American Commerce, or rather American SMUGGLING, to the Spanish Colonies. We entered into the LATTER for the defence of the Colonists; we carried it on for their security; and terminated it for their SOLE advantage. The two last Wars have cost this Country, at a moderate computation, ONE HUNDRED AND FIFTY MILLIONS. To this extraordinary waste of treasure, what have the Colonies to oppose to balance the account? Is it a languid Commerce, which scarcely makes its returns once in three years?

We have heard much (indeed, a great deal too much) of this Commerce from factious men on both sides of the Atlantic. This is the mighty engine which they wield over the heads of the ignorant; the great bug-bear with which they terrify the timid. To estimate the value of the American trade with any degree of precision, is impossible. The accounts kept in the Customhouse are no authorities. When exports pay no duty, a door is opened to false entries. The vanity

vanity of fome Merchants, the intereft of others, too frequently induce them to magnify, beyond meafure, the quantity of their export trade. Befides, the mercantile abettors of American refiftance thought they ferved the Colonies, whilft they gratified their own private views. We may conclude, that the Commerce with North-America has been greatly over-rated, as the TOTAL LOSS of it has NOT affected this Kingdom. We ought, perhaps, to afcribe to ITS INSIGNIFICANCE what we are taught to attribute to an INCREASE in other channels of trade.

Like all monopolies, the Commerce with North-America, fuch as it has been, was much more profitable to the Merchant, than advantageous to the Manufacturer. One-third of this commerce with any State in Europe (from which the returns are annual) would have brought equal profit to the manufacturer, and would have enabled him to employ an equal number of hands. Political impoftors will not fail to advance magnificent fictions on this head, and the ignorant cannot ceafe to give them credit. On a fubject where proofs are fo difficult to be obtained, one may hazard a conjecture. The money expended by this Nation upon America,

for

for the PROTECTION of HER inhabitants and the ENCOURAGEMENT of HER Commerce, would have been more than sufficient to purchase ALL the manufactures ever exported from Great-Britain to the Colonies now in rebellion. I mean not to include, in this conjectural estimate, any sums expended by us in any OTHER part of the world during the two last (truly American) Wars.

The Americans, with a degree of folly scarce excuseable in the most consummate ignorance, claim a merit with Great-Britain, for the Revenue arising from imposts laid upon some of their commodities, in THIS Kingdom. The chief of these are Rice and Tobacco. The Revenue arising from Rice is so insignificant, that it scarce deserves to be mentioned. It never amounted, at the highest computation, to ten thousand pounds in any one year. Tobacco, when re-exported, pays no duty; and it is a matter of great doubt, whether the frauds committed in the drawbacks may not nearly balance the ostensible Revenue arising to the State from the home consumption.

But

But, granting a great Revenue should arise from Rice and Tobacco to the State, what favour do we owe to our Colonies on that head? That Revenue is paid by OURSELVES. The Tax is on the Consumer, and not upon the Planter. Should Siberia supply us with Rice and Tobacco, the price would not probably be greater to the Consumer, nor the Revenue less to the State. If the Americans claim any merit from those Taxes, what do we NOT owe to the Emperor of China? The Revenue from Tea is much more considerable than that from Rice and Tobacco. A Congress at Pekin might accuse us of ingratitude on this subject, with as much justice as the Assembly lately sitting at Philadelphia.

It is evident, from the above state of facts, that the Colonies have no claim to an exemption from Taxation, on account of any advantage that has accrued to this country from their commerce. But Taxation has now ceased to be any part of the dispute. It goes to the whole authority of the Mother-Country. The Americans offer no longer the very name of Obedience. But why should I speak of Obedience? This VERY CONGRESS, whose Declaration is the subject of this disquisition, have passed

a VOTE

[81]

a VOTE OF INDEPENDENCE[*]. They have long acted as rebels, they NOW affect to contend as enemies. Their abettors in this Kingdom are no strangers to this circumstance; yet they dignify avowed rebellion with the title of "A GLORIOUS STRUGGLE FOR FREEDOM."

Such is the conduct of the Americans, to which that of Great-Britain has all along formed a striking contrast. With the indulgence and patience of a Parent, she soothed, flattered, and even courted them to a reconciliation. In pity to the weakness, in condescension to the folly, in consideration to the prejudices of a froward child, she held out the olive-branch, when she ought, perhaps, to have stretched forth the rod of correction. Her pity, her

---

[*] When this Vote was carried, the Provinces stood as follows:

For Independence.	Against it.
Massachuset'sBay	New York
Connecticut	New Jersey
New-Hampshire	Lower Counties
Pennsylvania	North Carolina
Virginia	Maryland.
South-Carolina	
Rhode-Island.	

This was the State of the Vote, on the first day. But, on the second day, Mr. Dickenson, AFTER REFLECTION ON HIS PILLOW, retracted, and carried off the Pennsylvania Delegates. There being then an equality of voices, the question *went off*, for the time.

M   kindness,

kindness, and affection, were lost upon the Americans. They advanced rapidly from claim to claim, and construed her forbearance into timidity. Each Act that was repealed furnished a subject for triumph, and not an object for gratitude. Each concession became the foundation of some new demand, till, at length, by assuming all to themselves by rebellion, they left the Mother-Country nothing to bestow.

In this situation of affairs, Great-Britain must pursue one of two lines of conduct, with regard to her refractory Colonies. She must either put up with the loss of ALL her expence, and emancipate them for ever, or reduce them to that state of dependence which subjects owe to the supreme authority in every Empire. As the latter line must of necessity be pursued, it ought to be pursued with a mixture of spirit and prudence. To be in every respect in a condition to force equitable terms, is the best security for their being voluntarily offered. But should terms be offered by the rebels, the RIGHTS OF THIS COUNTRY must be more regarded in the accommodation, than the CLAIMS of AMERICA. To permit the Colonies to GAIN by one rebellion, is to sow the seeds of another. But if the Colonies, as communities, are not permitted to *gain* by their refractory conduct, I am far from wishing that individuals should *lose* any part of their rights as British subjects.

To propose a plan to the Americans, in their present political frenzy, would be to speak to the winds. To make them *less* free than the other subjects of the State, can never be the *design* of this Country. To obtain *greater* privileges, can scarcely be their own *design*. If they are not madly bent on independence, let them propose the conditions on which they wish to continue subjects. But if they are to continue subjects, they must perform their duty as such, and contribute toward the expence of the State, for the general protection. The Legislature of this Kingdom cannot possibly depart from any part of its supremacy over the Colonies; but it is in the power of the Colonies to share in that supremacy. If they complain of being taxed without having the privilege of sending Members to Parliament, let them be represented. Nay, more: Let their representation increase in proportion to the Revenue they shall furnish. If they wish rather to vote their QUOTA towards the general supply, through their own General Courts and Assemblies, the resolution of Parliament on that subject is still open to their choice.

But as long as they assume the language of a Sovereign State, this Kingdom can enter into no negociation, can meet no compromise. Nations, as well as individuals, have a character, a certain dignity, which they must preserve at the risque of their existence. Great-Britain has obeyed the dictates of humanity beyond the limits prescribed by her reputation. To tempt her further, is full of peril, as her indignation begins to rise. She has long had reason to complain of American ingratitude; and she will not bear longer with American injustice. The dangerous resentment of a great people is ready to burst forth. They already begin to ask, with vehemence, Is this the return we ought to expect from Colonies, whom with parental indulgence we have cherished in infancy, protected in youth, and reared to manhood? Have we spent in their cause so much treasure, and have they the ingratitude to refuse to bear a small portion of our burdens? Have we spilt so much of the blood of their enemies, and do they repay us by imbruing their hands in our own? The law of God and of Nature is on the side of an indulgent Parent, against an undutiful Child; and should necessary correction render him incapable of future offence, he has only his own obstinacy and folly to blame.

[85]

An ACCOUNT of MONEY Voted for the FORCES employed in the Defence of AMERICA since the ACCESSION of the FAMILY of HANOVER; distinguishing each YEAR.

Year	£	s.	d.	Year	£	s.	d.
1714	39,478	11	0	1745	97,739	5	5
1715	34,742	14	2	1746	97,038	7	11
1716	34,837	17	10½	1747	97,038	7	11
1717	34,742	14	2	1748	97,277	2	6
1718	40,283	15	11	1749	63,002	17	1
1719	37,325	2	1	1750	81,059	14	2
1720	37,423	1	10½	1751	81,059	14	2
1721	40,396	9	7	1752	78,838	18	7
1722	40,396	9	7	1753	81,059	14	2
1723	40,396	9	7	1754	81,059	14	2
1724	40,502	17	8	1755	81,059	14	2
1725	40,396	9	7	1756	142,813	15	7½
1726	40,396	9	7	1757	249,854	1	3
1727	40,396	9	7	1758	449,094	4	7
1728	40,502	17	8	1759	445,013	9	7
1729	40,396	9	7	1760	482,797	8	6½
1730	40,396	9	7	1761	583,892	18	9
1731	40,396	9	7	1762	615,845	12	11
1732	40,502	17	8	1763	310,317	0	8
1733	40,396	9	7	1764	252,093	15	11½
1734	41,041	6	3	1765	268,054	19	9½
1735	52,754	15	5	1766	268,565	19	9½
1736	52,895	0	8	1767	279,668	1	5½
1737	52,754	15	5	1768	270,666	2	6½
1738	63,026	9	7	1769	269,615	2	3½
1739	65,106	19	7	1770	259,062	12	7½
1740	73,469	11	10½	1771	2⋅⋅,909	3	1½
1741	72,723	18	9	1772	263,650	5	6½
1742	74,027	8	9	1773	269,196	17	8½
1743	73,827	8	9	1774	247,324	5	2½
1744	81,595	19	8	1775	247,506	15	2½
	1,487,340	0	7¼		7,437,236	1	7

The

	£.	s.	d.
The Sums granted for the extraordinary Expences of the Army, Forts, Ordnance Stores, Transports, Carriages, Provisions, are so much dispersed through the Accounts of the various Offices, that it was found very difficult, if not impossible, to extract the particulars. The general Estimate is - - - - - - - -	8,779,925	3	$11\frac{3}{4}$
The same Observation may be made with regard to the Navy. The Expences of the Ships employed in North-America, are so much blended with the other Expences of the Navy, that it is impossible to separate them. At the most moderate Computation they may be estimated at - - - - - -	10,000,000	0	0
Money laid out in Indian Presents, in holding Congresses, and in purchasing cessions of land, may be estimated at -	610,000	0	0

An Account of Bounties on American Commodities.

	£.	s.	d.
Bounty on Indico from 1749 to 1773 paid by Great Britain - - -	145,022	3	$4\frac{1}{2}$
Bounty on Hemp and Flax paid under the Act of 4 Geo. III. ch. 26. from 1766 to 1772 - - - - - -	5,560	8	$7\frac{3}{4}$
Bounty on Importation of Naval Stores from America, pursuant to the Act of the 3d of Queen Anne, from 1706 to 1729	430,178	4	6
Under the Act of 2d Geo. II. from 1729 to 1774 - - - - -	1,028,584	7	3
	1,609,345	3	$9\frac{1}{4}$

Besides other Bounties granted on
    Raw Silk,
    Pipe Staves
    Hogshead Staves,
    Barrel Staves,
    Pipe, Hogshead, or Barrel-Heading

Total of Money laid out by Great-Britain on the Revolted Provinces, since the Accession of the House of Hanover -	34,697,142	10	$10\frac{1}{2}$

ACTS *establishing the* SUPREMACY *of* PARLIAMENT *over* AMERICA.

1. By 12 Ch. II. ch. 18, anno 1660. Tobacco not to be transported from America, except to England, or Plantations belonging to his Majesty, under the penalty of forfeiting ship and goods, &c.

2. By 15 Ch. II. No European goods to be imported into any of the Plantations, except on English-built ships, whereof the master and three-fourths of the men are English.----Duty laid on sea-coals sent to the Plantations, by the 10th section of said Act.

By 22 and 23 Ch. II. Plantation goods not to be carried to Ireland, and penalties inflicted for unloading them, otherwise than in England.

3. By 25th Ch. II. The exportation of Plantation commodities farther restrained.

4. By 13 and 14 Ch. II. sec. 12. Same restraints extend to Molasses and Rice.

By 7 and 8 Wm. III. sec. 16. An Act for preventing Frauds, and regulating the Plantation-trade—Section 15 prohibits any body, claiming lands by Charter or Letters-patent on the Continent of America, from selling their property to any person, otherwise than natural-born subjects of England, Ireland, Wales, and Town of Berwick upon Tweed, without the consent of his Majesty, heirs, and successors.

By 7 and 8 Wm. III. sec. 6. Officers of Customs to have the same power in America, as in England.---Sec. 9 directs that all By-laws and Customs in America contrary to said Act, or any other Act to be made in England, shall be void.

8 Geo. I. ch. 15. sec. 24. Furs required to be brought from the Plantations to Great Britain.

5 G. II. ch. 7. Lands in the Plantations made liable to the payment of Debts.

5 G. II. ch. 22. Hats not to be exported from one Plantation to another.

13 Geo. II. ch. 7. Naturalizing all Foreigners, even Jews, who shall reside seven years in the Colonies.

ACTS *complained of by the* AMERICANS.
IN *Mr.* GRENVILLE'S *Administration.*

4 G. III. ch. 34. Paper Bills in the Plantations declared void.

UNDER *the Administration of Lord* ROCKINGHAM *and the Duke of* GRAFTON.

6. Geo. III. c. 2. The declaratory Act of the Supremacy of Great-Britain.

7 G. III. ch. 41. Customs and Duties in the British Colonies put under the management of the Commissioners residing there.

UNDER *the Administration of Lord* CHATHAM *and the Duke of* GRAFTON.

7 Geo. III. c. 59. Suspending all proceedings of the Council of New York, till provision be made for the British troops.

8 Geo. III. ch. 22. Act for more easy recovery of Penalties inflicted by the Acts relating to Trade, and the Revenues in the Plantations.

ACTS *of* PARLIAMENT *for imposing Taxes on* America.

12 Ch. II. ch. 4. Tonnage and Poundage extended to all his Majesty's Dominions, without exception.

25 Ch. II. ch. 7. sec. 2. If Bonds are not given to land the goods imported from America, in England, &c. then several duties to be imposed, collected under the direction of the Officers of the Customs in England.

9 Ann. ch. 10.—Post-Office.

9 Ann. ch. 27. Lays a duty on Prize goods carried to America.

3 Geo. II. ch. 28. sec. 25. The Half-Subsidy to be paid on Rice from Carolina to Cape Finisterre—8 Geo. II. ch. 19. The same extended to Georgia, and continued down by subsequent Acts.

6 Geo. II. ch. 13. Upon the Importation of Rum, Sugar, and Molasses into America, several duties to be paid.

ACTS *complained of by the* AMERICANS.

IN *Mr.* GRENVILLE's *Administration.*

4 Geo. III. ch. 15. Certain Rates and Duties on foreign goods imported into the Colonies.

5 Geo. III. Postage of Letters.

IN *the Administration of Lord* CHATHAM *and the Duke of* GRAFTON.

6 Geo. III. ch. 52. Alterations made in the Act of the 4th of Geo. III.

7 Geo. III. ch. 46. Duties laid on the importation of certain goods imported into the Colonies.

UNDER *Lord* NORTH's *Administration.*

10 Geo. III. The above Act repealed, except as to Tea.

A

DECLARATION

BY THE

REPRESENTATIVES

OF THE

UNITED COLONIES OF NORTH AMERICA,

NOW MET IN

GENERAL CONGRESS AT PHILADELPHIA,

SETTING FORTH

THE CAUSES AND NECESSITY OF THEIR TAKING UP ARMS.

IF it was poffible for men who exercife their reafon to believe, that the Divine Author of our exiftence intended a part of the human race to hold an abfolute property in, and an unbounded power over others, marked out by his infinite goodnefs and wifdom as the objects of a legal domination, never rightfully refiftible, however fevere and oppreffive; the inhabitants of thefe Colonies might at leaft require from the Parliament of Great Britain fome evidence, that this dreadful authority over them has been granted to that body. But a reverence for our Great Creator, principles of humanity, and the dictates of common fenfe, muft convince all thofe who reflect upon the fubject, that Government was inftituted to promote the welfare of mankind, and ought to be adminiftered administered for the attainment of that end. The Legislature of Great Britain, however, stimulated by an inordinate passion for a power not only unjustifiable, but which they know to be peculiarly reprobated by the very constitution of that Kingdom, and desperate of success in any mode of contest, where regard should be had to truth, law, or right, have at length, deserting those, attempted to effect their cruel and impolitic purpose of enslaving these Colonies by violence, and have thereby rendered it necessary for us to close with their last appeal from reason to arms.---Yet, however blinded that Assembly may be, by their intemperate rage for unlimited domination, so to slight justice and the opinion of mankind, we esteem ourselves bound by obligations of respect to the rest of the world, to make known the justice of our cause.

Our forefathers, inhabitants of the island of Great Britain, left their native land, to seek on these shores a residence for civil and religious freedom. At the expence of their blood, at the hazard of their fortunes, without the least charge to the country from which they removed, by unceasing labour, and an unconquerable spirit, they effected settlements in the distant and inhospitable wilds of America, then filled with numerous and warlike nations of barbarians. Societies or governments, vested with perfect legislatures, were formed under Charters from the Crown, and an harmonious intercourse was established between the Colonies and the Kingdom from which they derived their origin. The mutual benefits of this union became in a short time so extraordinary, as to excite astonishment. It is universally confessed, that the amazing increase of the wealth, strength, and navigation of the realm arose from this source; and the Minister who so wisely and successfully directed the measures of Great Britain in the late war, publickly declared, that these Colonies enabled her to triumph over her enemies. ---Towards the conclusion of that war it pleased our Sovereign to make a change in his Councils.---From that fatal moment the affairs of the British Empire began to fall into confusion, and gradually sliding from the summit of glorious prosperity, to which they had

been

been advanced by the virtues and abilities of one man, are at length distracted by the convulsions that now shake it to its deepest foundation. The new Ministry finding the brave foes of Britain, though frequently defeated, yet still contending, took up the unfortunate idea of granting them a hasty peace, and of then subduing her faithful friends.

These devoted Colonies were judged to be in such a state, as to present victories without bloodshed, and all the easy emoluments of statuteable plunder. The uninterrupted tenor of their peaceable and respectful behaviour from the beginning of Colonization, their dutiful, zealous, and useful services during the war, tho' so recently and amply acknowledged in the most honourable manner by his Majesty, by the late King, and by Parliament, could not save them from the meditated innovations. Parliament was influenced to adopt the pernicious project, and assuming a new power over them, have, in the course of eleven years, given such decisive specimens of the spirit and consequences attending this power, as to leave no doubt concerning the effects of acquiescence under it. They have undertaken to give and grant our money without our consent, tho' we have ever exercised an exclusive right to dispose of our own property. Statutes have been passed for extending the jurisdiction of Courts of Admiralty and Vice-Admiralty beyond their antient limits, for depriving us of the accustomed and inestimable privilege of trial by Jury in cases affecting both life and property; for suspending the legislature of one of the Colonies; for interdicting all commerce of another; and for altering fundamentally the form of government, established by charter, and secured by Acts of its own Legislature solemnly confirmed by the Crown; for exempting the "Murderers" of Colonists from legal trial, and, in effect, from punishment; for erecting in a neighbouring Province, acquired by the joint arms of Great Britain and America, a despotism dangerous to our very existence; and for quartering soldiers upon the Colonists in time of profound peace. It has also been resolved in Parliament, that Colonists charged with committing certain

certain offences, shall be transported to England to be tried.

But why should we enumerate our injuries in detail? By one Statute it is declared, that Parliament can "of right make laws to bind us in all cases whatsoever." What is to defend us against so enormous, so unlimited a power? Not a single man of those who assume it, is chosen by us, or is subject to our controul or influence; but, on the contrary, they are all of them exempt from the operation of such laws; and an American revenue, if not diverted from the ostensible purposes for which it is raised, would actually lighten their own burdens in proportion as they increase ours. We saw the misery to which such despotism would reduce us. We for ten years incessantly and ineffectually besieged the Throne as supplicants; we reasoned, we remonstrated with Parliament in the most mild and decent language. But Administration, sensible that we should regard these oppressive measures as freemen ought to do, sent over fleets and armies to enforce them. The indignation of the Americans was roused, it is true; but it was the indignation of a virtuous, loyal, and affectionate people. A Congress of Delegates from the United Colonies was assembled at Philadelphia, on the 5th day of last September. We resolved again to offer an humble and dutiful Petition to the King, and also addressed our fellow-subjects of Great-Britain. We have pursued every temperate, every respectful measure; we have even proceeded to break off our commercial intercourse with our fellow-subjects, as the last peaceable admonition, that our attachment to no nation upon earth should supplant our attachment to liberty. This we flattered ourselves was the ultimate step of the controversy; but the subsequent events have shewn, how vain is this hope of finding moderation in our enemies.

Several threatening expressions against the Colonies were inserted in his Majesty's Speech. Our Petition, though we were told it was a decent one, that his Majesty had been pleased to receive it graciously, and to promise laying it before his Parliament, was huddled into

to both Houses amongst a bundle of American papers, and there neglected. The Lords and Commons in their Address, in the month of February, said, That "a rebellion at that time actually existed within the Province of Massachuset's Bay; and that those concerned in it had been countenanced and encouraged by unlawful combinations and engagements, entered into by his Majesty's subjects in several of the other Colonies; and therefore they besought his Majesty, that he would take the most effectual measures to enforce due obedience to the laws and authority of the Supreme Legislature." Soon after the commercial intercourse of whole Colonies, with foreign countries, and with each other, was cut off by an Act of Parliament; by another, several of them were entirely prohibited from the fisheries in the seas near their coasts, on which they always depended for their sustenance; and large reinforcements of ships and troops were immediately sent over to General Gage.

Fruitless were all the entreaties, arguments and eloquence of an illustrious band of the most distinguished Peers and Commoners, who nobly and strenuously asserted the justice of our cause, to stay or even to mitigate the heedless fury with which these accumulated and unexampled outrages were hurried on. Equally fruitless was the interference of the City of London, of Bristol, and many other respectable towns, in our favour. Parliament adopted an insidious manoeuvre, calculated to divide us, to establish a perpetual auction of taxations, where Colony should bid against Colony, all of them uninformed what ransom should redeem their lives, and thus to extort from us, at the point of the bayonet, the unknown sums that should be sufficient to gratify, if possible to gratify, Ministerial rapacity, with the miserable indulgence left to us of raising in our own mode the prescribed tribute. What terms more rigid and humiliating could have been dictated by remorseless victors to conquered enemies? In our circumstances, to accept them would be to deserve them.

Soon after the intelligence of these proceedings arrived on this Continent, General Gage, who in the course of the

the last year had taken possession of the town of Boston, in the province of Massachuset's-Bay, and still occupied it as a garrison, on the 19th day of April sent out from that place a large detachment of his army, who made an unprovoked assault on the inhabitants of the said province, at the town of Lexington, as appears by the affidavits of a great number of persons, some of whom were officers and soldiers of that detachment, murdered eight of the inhabitants, and wounded many others. From thence the troops proceeded in warlike array to the town of Concord, where they set upon another party of the inhabitants of the same Province, killing several, and wounded more, until compelled to retreat by the country people suddenly assembled to repel this cruel aggression. Hostilities thus commenced by the British troops, have been since prosecuted by them without regard to faith or reputation. The inhabitants of Boston being confined within that town by the General their Governor, and having in order to procure their dismission entered into a treaty with him, it was stipulated that the said inhabitants, having deposited their arms with their own Magistrates, should have liberty to depart, taking with them their other effects. They accordingly delivered up their arms; but in open violation of honour, in defiance of the obligation of treaties, which even savage nations esteem sacred, the Governor ordered the arms deposited as aforesaid, that they might be preserved for their owners, to be seized by a body of soldiers; detained the greatest part of the inhabitants in the town, and compelled the few who were permitted to retire, to leave their most valuable effects behind.

By this perfidy wives are separated from their husbands, children from their parents, the aged and sick from their relations and friends, who wish to attend and comfort them; and those who have been used to live in plenty, and even elegance, are reduced to deplorable distress.

The General, further emulating his Ministerial masters, by a proclamation, bearing date on the 12th day of June, after venting the grossest falsehoods and calumnies against the good people of these Colonies, proceeds
to

to "declare them all, either by name or description, to be rebels and traitors, to supersede the course of the common law, and instead thereof to publish and order the use and exercise of the law martial."——His troops have butchered our countrymen; have wantonly burnt Charles Town, besides a considerable number of houses in other places; our ships and vessels are seized; the necessary supplies of provisions are intercepted, and he is exerting his utmost power to spread destruction and devastation around him.

We have received certain intelligence, that General Carleton, the Governor of Canada, is instigating the people of that Province and the Indians to fall upon us; and we have but too much reason to apprehend, that schemes have been formed to excite domestic enemies against us. In brief, a part of these Colonies now feels, and all of them are sure of feeling, as far as the vengeance of Administration can inflict them, the complicated calamities of fire, sword and famine. We are reduced to the alternative of chusing an unconditional submission to the tyranny of irritated Ministers, or resistance by force. The latter is our choice. We have counted the cost of this contest, and find nothing so dreadful as voluntary slavery. Honour, justice and humanity, forbid us tamely to surrender that freedom which we received from our gallant ancestors, and which our innocent posterity have a right to receive from us. We cannot endure the infamy and guilt of resigning succeeding generations to that wretchedness which inevitably awaits them, if we basely entail hereditary bondage upon them.

Our cause is just: our union is perfect: our internal resources are great, and if necessary, foreign assistance is undoubtedly attainable. We gratefully acknowledge, as signal instances of Divine favour towards us, that his Providence would not permit us to be called into this severe controversy, until we were grown up to our present strength, had been previously exercised in warlike operations, and possessed of the means of defending ourselves. With hearts fortified with these animating reflections, we most solemnly before God and the world declare, that, exerting the utmost energy of those powers which our beneficent Creator hath graciously bestowed upon us,

[25]

the arms we have been compelled by our enemies to assume, we will, in defiance of every hazard, with unabating firmness and perseverance, employ for the preservation of our liberties, being with one mind resolved to die freemen rather than to live slaves.

Lest this Declaration should disquiet the minds of our friends and fellow-subjects in any part of the empire, we assure them, that we mean not to dissolve that union which has so long and so happily subsisted between us, and which we sincerely wish to see restored.—Necessity has not yet driven us into that desperate measure, or induced us to excite any other nation to war against them. We have not raised armies with ambitious designs of separating from Great-Britain, and establishing independant states. We fight not for glory or for conquest. We exhibit to mankind the remarkable spectacle of a people attacked by unprovoked enemies, without any imputation or even suspicion of offence. They boast of their privileges and civilization, and yet proffer no milder conditions than servitude or death.

In our own native land, in defence of the freedom that is our birthright, and which we ever enjoyed till the late violation of it—for the protection of our property, acquired solely by the honest industry of our forefathers and ourselves, against violence actually offered, we have taken up arms. We shall lay them down when hostilities shall cease on the part of the aggressors, and all danger of their being renewed shall be removed, and not before.

With an humble confidence in the mercies of the Supreme and impartial Judge and Ruler of the Universe, we most devoutly implore his divine goodness to conduct us happily through this great conflict, to dispose our adversaries to reconciliation on reasonable terms, and thereby to relieve the Empire from the calamities of civil war.

By Order of Congress,

JOHN HANCOCK, President.

Attested,
CHARLES THOMPSON, Secretary.

Philadelphia, July 6, 1775.

www.ingramcontent.com/pod-product-compliance
Lightning Source LLC
Chambersburg PA
CBHW020900160426
43192CB00007B/1001